Memories
of
Northampton

True North Books Ltd
Elland
West Yorkshire
HX5 9AE

THE PUBLISHERS WOULD LIKE TO THANK THE
FOLLOWING COMPANIES FOR SUPPORTING THE
PRODUCTION OF THIS BOOK

MAIN SPONSOR
CHURCH'S CHINA

BRITISH TIMKEN LIMITED
CARLSBERG-TETLEY BREWING LIMITED
CHURCH'S SHOES
COUNTRY LION (NORTHAMPTON) LIMITED
R GRIGGS GROUP LIMITED
W GROSE LIMITED
THE GROSVENOR SHOPPING CENTRE
HAWES SIGNS LIMITED
HAYNES & CANN LIMITED
HEWITSON BECKE & SHAW
THE HOSPITALS GUILD
MICHAEL JONES JEWELLER
FG METCALFE & SON LIMITED
NORTHAMPTON COLLEGE
NENE UNIVERSITY COLLEGE
OLIVER ADAMS LIMITED
W PEARCE & CO (NORTHAMPTON) LIMITED
QUINTON HOUSE SCHOOL
SHEINMAN OPTICIANS
WARDLE & KEACH LIMITED
WESTON FAVELL SHOPPING CENTRE
WILCON HOMES LIMITED

First published in Great Britain by True North Books Limited
Units 3 - 5 Heathfield Industrial Park
Elland West Yorkshire
HX5 9AE
Tel. 01422 377977

ISBN 1 900463 48 2

Introduction

'Do you remember when....' is a phrase often heard today, and in response to the ever-increasing demand for local nostalgia we are pleased to be able to introduce Memories of Northampton. In page after page of nostalgic images the book gives readers an entertaining glimpse back through the years at how people used to shop, work and play in the days that seem like only yesterday.

Many books of local history and nostalgic photographs already exist, of course, but the thing that sets Memories of Northampton apart is the fact that it is packed with images taken from a period within living memory, chosen according to their ability to rekindle fond memories of how people used to shop, work and play in the area where they grew up.

This is not a book about crinolines or bowler-hats! Local companies and organisations have allowed us to study their archives and include their history - and fascinating reading it makes. We are pleased to be able to make it possible for them to share their achievements with a wider audience.

The book has far more to do with entertainment than serious study, but we hope you will agree it is none the worse for that. Modern image reproduction techniques have enabled us to present these pictures in a way rarely seen before, and we have attempted to set the book apart by means of lively design and generous and informative text.

It is hoped that the following pages will prompt readers' own memories of Northampton from days gone by - and we are always delighted to hear from people who can add to the information contained in the captions so that we can enhance future editions of the book. Memories of Northampton has been a pleasure to compile, we sincerely hope you enjoy reading it.

Happy memories!

Text, design and origination by True North Books Limited, Elland, West Yorkshire
Printed and bound by The Amadeus Press Limited, Huddersfield, West Yorkshire

Contents

Around the town centre

It is a fairly quiet time of day in the Market Square sometime in the 1950s. In the foreground the sections of the stalls are about to go up, or perhaps they have just come down. At any rate the few people about are not enough to disturb the pigeons from roaming freely. Some of the names on the buildings would have been familiar enough at this time, from Roses Fashion Centre and Phoenix Assurance in the rear, to Pearl Assurance and Liptons to the right. In the middle distance, the striking tower of All Saints Church dominates the skyline. There are one or two interesting vehicles on view, including a Morris Traveller in the foreground and some which look more like 'pocket battleships' to the rear. Also a 'Player's Weights' advertisement, on the side of an old van to the right, is an eye-catcher. Nevertheless, with the square clear of stalls, the eye is inevitably drawn to the focal point, the magnificent fountain on its plinth at the centre. This was made locally and presented to the town in 1863 by Samuel Isaacs to commemorate the marriage of Albert Edward, Prince of Wales, to Princess Alexandra of Denmark.

Above: A modest sized petrol tanker (by modern standards) is rumbling its way across South Bridge and its appearance, linked with the style of the other vehicles on view, would place this photograph as no later than the 1950s. Some interesting buildings are on view including, in the distance, the two breweries of P Phipps & Co and the Northamptonshire Brewery Company. Smell can be as powerfully evocative as sight or sound and once experienced that tang of hops in the air can never be forgotten. The tall building just beyond the petrol tanker has the inscription EAGLE FOUNDRY just below the triangular pediment. This was originally Rice's Foundry. A quick glance at the structure on the left shows that it has some fine architectural features. Although it carries an advertisement for Phipps as brewers, malsters and wine and spirit merchants, it was in fact a warehouse, not a brewery. Because it was a listed structure, a later proposal to develop it was refused planning permission. Soon afterwards it was burned down in mysterious circumstances and this constituted a great visual loss to this part of Northampton.

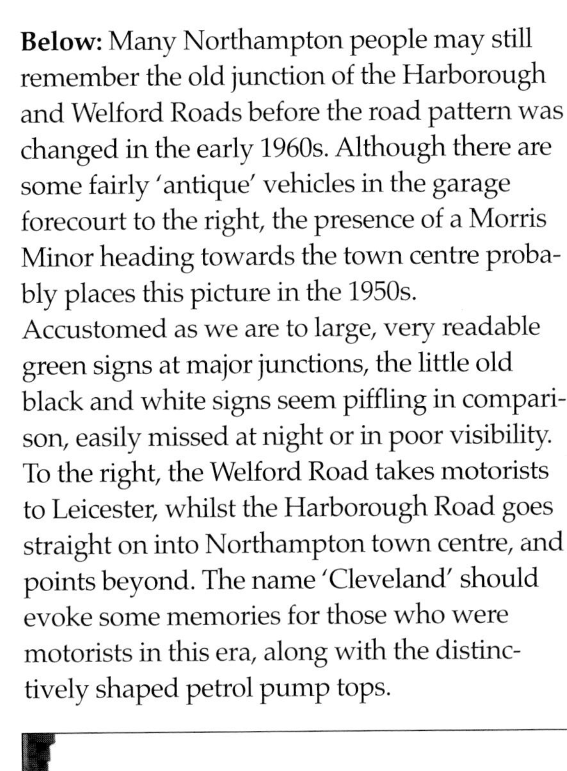

Below: Many Northampton people may still remember the old junction of the Harborough and Welford Roads before the road pattern was changed in the early 1960s. Although there are some fairly 'antique' vehicles in the garage forecourt to the right, the presence of a Morris Minor heading towards the town centre probably places this picture in the 1950s. Accustomed as we are to large, very readable green signs at major junctions, the little old black and white signs seem piffling in comparison, easily missed at night or in poor visibility. To the right, the Welford Road takes motorists to Leicester, whilst the Harborough Road goes straight on into Northampton town centre, and points beyond. The name 'Cleveland' should evoke some memories for those who were motorists in this era, along with the distinctively shaped petrol pump tops. No such thing as self-service pumps in those days. You were likely to be served by somebody wiping their hands on an oily rag who would have given you a very funny look if you had asked for crisps and chocolates as well! It was a nice touch to thank customers in such a prominent way, but the garage was to disappear in the changes to come.

Bottom: Marefair in the 1950s presents a rather gloomy and wet scene but it preserves an image that would otherwise only exist in memory. The whole of the north or left-hand side has been developed into the massive Barclaycard complex, but the imposing structure in the photograph had a rich and varied history. The North Western Hotel sign can be clearly seen, but the building had been the Rose and Punchbowl Hotel before the London, North Western Railway took it over. The building itself is a fine example of the architecture of a bygone age, with an eye-catching style and symmetry, not least the roof gables with their ornamental tops. The street scene below the windows of the hotel is rather mundane, although the link with the railways is maintained by the three-wheeled railway mechanical horse approaching in the distance. The Morris Minor coming up the street helps to set the scene in the 1950s.

Above: A variety of shops and little businesses, along with some interesting architectural styles, would have greeted your eye as you progressed down Newland into Market Square in 1958. The shop with the Castrol sign on the far left had been the Goff & Lee cycle shop, but at this date belonged to Andre Baldet. Across Princess Street stood the old Temperance Hall Cinema, and its sign is clear to be seen on the attractive frontage overlooking Newland. A little further down the left-hand side of the street would have found you at the Popular Café, whilst just around the corner was the historic Welsh house. This was playing host to a garage and a school of motoring in 1958. A splendid Austin Princess makes an appearance on the far right, whilst further down the street the CIU sign invites you to slake your thirst at the Century Club, an imposing Working Men's Club. The 'Chronicle & Echo' van is parked at the rear entrance of the newspaper offices. In the background across Market Square, Roses Fashion Centre, in Waterloo House, catches the eye.

By 1972 this part of Newland had been swept away as part of the Grosvenor Centre development.

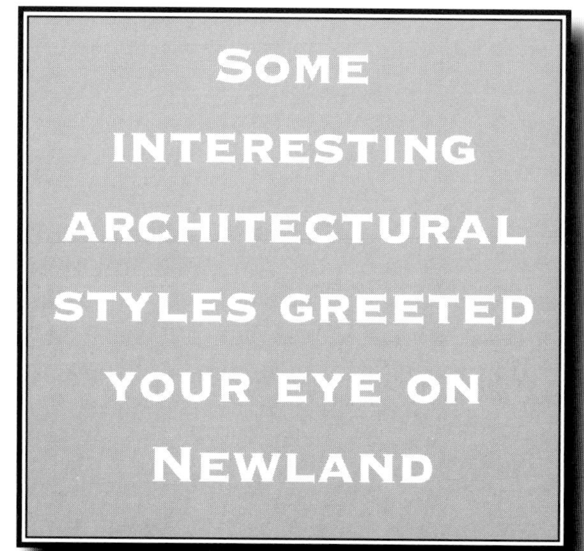

Right: It may be going to work time or coming home time; either way it's a fairly busy time on Horseshoe Street sometime in the 1950s. The gaslamps put the picture in that decade, as do the vehicles on display. It may be a little milk float that has edged over to the wrong side of the road, behind the van. Whatever it is, there may be problems for the two cyclists if they come round the corner too fast. In some ways the brightest spots on the photograph are the billboards. Their advertisements illuminate what otherwise appears to be a rather grey day. Some of the products advertised have stood the test of time, and some familiar names are there. However, whatever happened to Tide, seemingly 'loved by women' and 'the greatest wash of all'? Perhaps it went to the Great Washing-Machine in the Sky, along with other old favourites such as Omo and Oxydol, to be replaced by brands that are even greater than 'greatest.' Horseshoe Street had the wonderfully named Gasometer Public House on its right hand side, but the construction of the huge traffic junction in this area has now placed this scene in the nostalgia category.

Below: Town and city centres are constantly under a process of change and this part of Northampton has been transformed since this photograph of Newland was taken, not many years after the Second World War. There is some degree of modernity in that a one-way system has been instituted, but otherwise this image belongs very much to the past. Nevertheless many residents of Northampton will remember the familiar landmarks of the 'Chronicle and Echo' offices and the Century Club up the left-hand side of the street. There is a line of very solid looking vehicles parked down the right-hand side of Newland outside Dewhirsts and the Popular Café. Perhaps most interesting of all is the historic Welsh house at the bottom of Newland which, at this stage, accommodated a garage and a school of motoring. The inscription (to the right of the garage sign) is in Welsh and translates as, 'Without God Nothing. With God Enough.' The whole of this part of Newland was swept away in changes that created the Grosvenor Centre Shopping Mall in 1972. However, in a curious sort of way, the old Welsh house survived, for a replica of the building was constructed and incorporated into the new development.

Below: A New Theatre enclosed by scaffolding, and on the verge of complete demolition, is the sad theme of this 1960 photograph. How could this living theatre have died? Perhaps it was the rise of the cinema. Film-going rose in popularity throughout the 1930s and peaked in the 40s and 50s. Many old music halls and variety theatres saw no other course of survival than to become cinemas themselves. The New Theatre had only a brief flirtation with films, between 1933 and 1934. Post-war audiences were sparse, in spite of the appearance of major entertainment figures such as John Gielgud, Claire Bloom, Arthur Askey and Jimmy Edwards. It was perhaps a desperate response to this that caused the management of the New Theatre to turn to strip shows in the 1950s. This had the effect of destroying the theatre's reputation for family entertainment as the locals dubbed it the 'Newd Theatre'. Strenuous attempts were made to save it but the last show before closure, in 1958, was 'Strip, Strip, Hooray', an ignominious end. An attempt was made to preserve the four stone urns on the parapet, and the photograph shows Mr Lou Warwick, the acknowledged expert on the New Theatre, as proud possessor of one of them.

Right: There's no going back now! Perhaps even the council planners, along with the supporters of the town centre redevelopment scheme, had a few qualms at this stage. Wood Street is in process of obliteration in 1972, part of the price paid for the building of the Grosvenor Shopping Centre. This is always the worst phase of any rebuilding scheme, when the area resembles a bomb site. Nothing much is left of the old; nothing recognisable has yet emerged of the new. It must have presented a gloomy picture even to those most fervently in favour of the project. There were plenty against it, of course, for the Grosvenor Centre scheme was nothing if not controversial. Undoubtedly many fine buildings and streets of character were reduced to the kind of rubble that is visible in the photograph. One can imagine too the noise of crashing masonry and billowing clouds of dust that are always attendant on the early stages of redevelopment. Perhaps the group of young ladies coming down the road had run the gauntlet of this on a daily basis. If so, they had seen Wood Street disappear before their very eyes.

Above: A bird's eye view from the high-rise flats in 'The Boroughs', the area of Spring Lane and Scarletwell Street, looks south-eastwards. The late 1950s and early 1960s saw redevelopment begin in earnest in the central areas of Northampton, and the block of flats from which this photograph was taken was the first of the high-rise structures. The immediate foreground view shows that more were to follow. The foundations of former buildings are visible on the left and the dilapidated state of the properties to the right, along with the heavy wagon's presence, show that demolition is imminent. The historic market space of the Mayorhold, to the right, was soon to disappear. Keeping to this side of the picture, the name of Nicholson Wool Merchant might be visible, arched over the door of the large warehouse. To the left of this, the white building is the King's Head public house. Clusters of buildings densely pack the middleground, interspersed with clumps of trees. At top left, the skyline is dominated by the spire of the Church of the Holy Sepulchre, whilst just right of centre may be seen the distant water tower of the Lotus shoe factory in Newland.

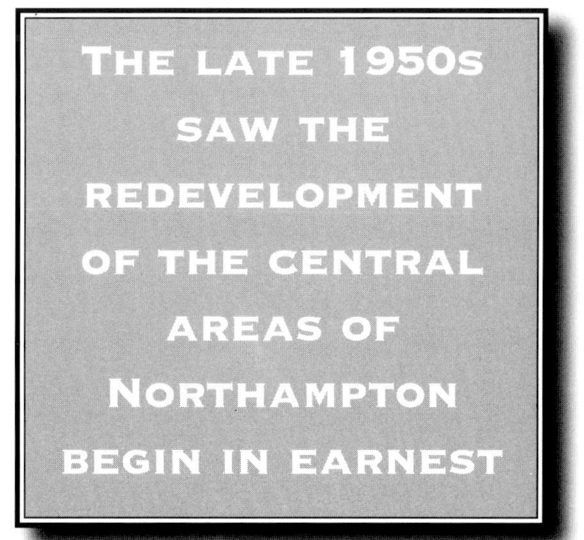

An elevated view looking east from Market Square finds Abington Street thronged with shoppers. Fashions and vehicles indicate the 1950s and the numbers of people about suggest a time of day when, only a few years later, the traffic would be nose-to-tail down the street. These were calmer times, however, as far as cars were concerned and freer movement was allowed after the bottleneck which had blighted the street had been demolished in 1946. The site on the corner of Dychurch Lane, to the right, had not yet been developed when this photograph was taken. Much of the interest in the picture lies on the right-hand side. Above Wiggins & Co Ltd is a round sign indicating the offices of Friends Provident and Century Insurance. This has a splendidly solid and old-fashioned ring about it, but it is the nostrils of the older readers which might quiver at the mention of Kingham's Grocers. This too was to be found in the block of buildings to the right and is best remembered for the aroma of roasting coffee which wafted out of it and along Abington Street.

Above: There was no missing the offices of the Northampton Gaslight Company which used to stand on the corner of Abington Street and Wellington Street. That the building was actually constructed for the Gas Company, rather than built for some other purpose, is revealed by the fact that 'GAS' is literally carved there in stone. It was certainly an imposing, not to say overpowering edifice, and no doubt hundreds of people found their daily employment there. Another person who must have found plenty of work there is the window cleaner whose handcart and ladders are parked outside the spacious entrance. The number of windows to be cleaned suggests that it was a very worthwhile contract. The handcart has a touch of nostalgia about it, for window cleaners tend to be motorised today. Again, the white-coated delivery boy cycling up the street with his basket to the fore is a rare sight now, and the scenario has a 1950s look about it. The Gas Company's building has that very functional look of 1930s architecture. If that is the case it did not have too long a lifespan, for it was demolished in 1969 to make way for a Marks and Spencer store.

Top: The H Samuel clock tells us that it is 11.18am in this 1950s shot of The Drapery from the top of Bridge Street, and this was one clock that just had to be right. The Drapery is impressively framed by the fine buildings of Boots and H Samuel to the left, and the imposing structure of the Westminster Bank to the right, complete with dome. The bus in the distance is of the old open-ended variety, which gave you a sporting chance of swinging onto the platform at the first corner if you had just missed it. A casual swinging off at a later stage was not just as easily accomplished, and sometimes ended in humiliation. Shoppers throng The Drapery, and the fact that it is a one-way street shows that the council had recognised the need for some sort of traffic control. The rise of the mass ownership of cars saw the germ of a problem in the 1950s reach acute proportions by the 1960s. Traffic congestion and hazardous fumes caused major difficulties in the centres of towns and cities. The answer lay in ring roads, large car parks and pedestrianised areas, such as The Drapery has now become.

THE FIFTY SHILLING TAILORS
HOWARD
AVV

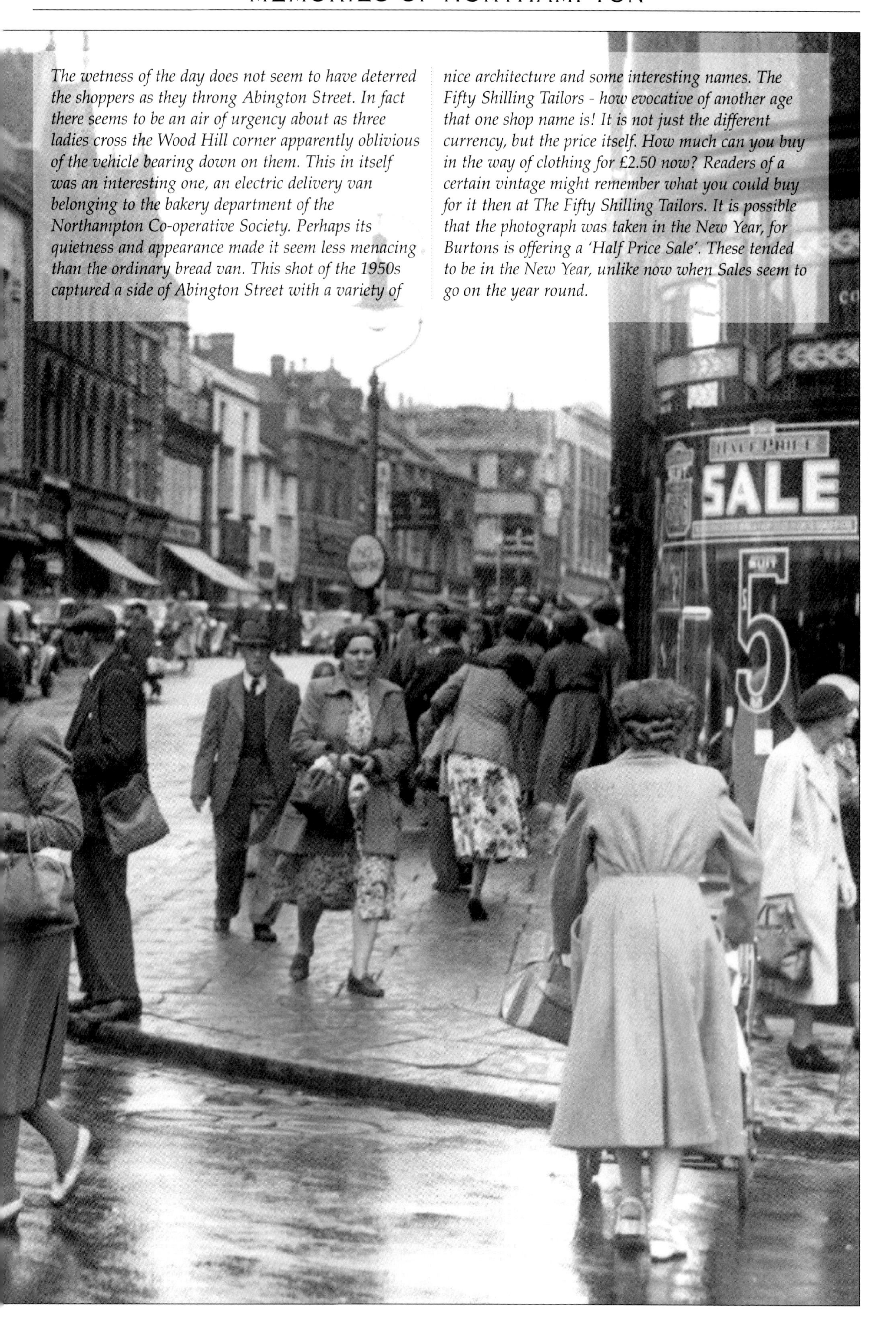

The wetness of the day does not seem to have deterred the shoppers as they throng Abington Street. In fact there seems to be an air of urgency about as three ladies cross the Wood Hill corner apparently oblivious of the vehicle bearing down on them. This in itself was an interesting one, an electric delivery van belonging to the bakery department of the Northampton Co-operative Society. Perhaps its quietness and appearance made it seem less menacing than the ordinary bread van. This shot of the 1950s captured a side of Abington Street with a variety of nice architecture and some interesting names. The Fifty Shilling Tailors - how evocative of another age that one shop name is! It is not just the different currency, but the price itself. How much can you buy in the way of clothing for £2.50 now? Readers of a certain vintage might remember what you could buy for it then at The Fifty Shilling Tailors. It is possible that the photograph was taken in the New Year, for Burtons is offering a 'Half Price Sale'. These tended to be in the New Year, unlike now when Sales seem to go on the year round.

Above: The dense urban pattern of St James' End is featured in this aerial shot of the 1960s. Castle Station and the goods yards are visible at bottom right as West Bridge straddles the waterway and lowlands into the St James area. The railway line is a prominent feature in this bottom corner, and the number of goods wagons is a reminder of how much freight was still carried by rail even in the 1960s. Foot Meadow is to be found in the bottom corner, and the industrial complex towards the bottom left is a foretaste of all the depots and warehouses that can be found on the flatlands off the photograph, down towards the River Nene and the Grand Junction Canal. At middle right of the photograph is Victoria Park, with its tennis courts and bowling green. Moving to the left off West Bridge one can follow St James' Road as it curves steadily round to the right. To the left of the road, as it begins to forge upwards, the factory signs of 'Moccasins' and 'Shoes for Men' are a reminder of the town's old staple industry. St James' Church itself is a little further up, to the right of the road.

Right: If London buses tend to travel in threes, then Northampton buses progress in convoys of nine or ten, might be the first impression given by this picture. In fact the queue of buses in Market Square was part of a Holidays at Home promotion by the Corporation Transport Department in the immediate post-war years. People had not been encouraged to travel during the Second World War. Petrol was in short supply and economy was the order of the day, as encapsulated in the government slogan, Is Your Journey Really Necessary? Things did not improve greatly even when the war was over and hence the Holidays at Home campaign. During Northampton's annual summer shoe holiday fortnight, those who still could not get away could at least enjoy entertainments put on by the Corporation. One of the diversions was a bus tour of the suburbs which were in the process of being developed after 1945. Apart from the line of buses in Market Square, an interesting array of old cars offers an identification challenge to automobile buffs. In the background the distinctive white facade of Burtons can be seen behind the buses, with Waterloo House to the far right.

BURTON
PEACOCK HOTEL
ATLAS ASSURANCE COMPANY
BURTON
SGB
SPECIAL

In the 1960s plenty of open spaces presented themselves in the Kingsthorpe area

Neat rows of houses and intersecting roads mark this aerial view of the Kingsthorpe area. The shot was taken on a sunny day in the 1960s and the shadows of trees and houses can clearly be seen. Kingsthorpe Road sweeps up from bottom left, with Kingsthorpe Grove joining it from bottom right. From the Y junction, in the middle of the picture, Welford Road branches off to the left whilst Harborough Road goes right. In the apex of that junction, an old garage was being demolished at the time of this photograph. Plenty of open spaces present themselves. At the top is the Recreation Ground, known locally as the 'big rec', with its playing fields, tennis courts and bowling greens. The 'little rec' can be located bottom right, between Cranford Road and Kingsland Avenue. For those who like a 'then and now' perspective, the area to the mid-left of the picture offers some scope. In the 1960s this contained a nursery, market gardens and the Ritz Cinema. It is now occupied by the Waitrose supermarket. What will it all look like forty years from now?

Towcester Road is the main highway across this aerial view of Far Cotton. Row upon row of neatly patterned Victorian terraces dominate the centre of the photograph, whilst in the foreground there is a more modern council estate. Just above this, on the right, is the large expanse of the recreation ground, with its tennis courts and bowling greens. Beyond the green space, the spire of St Mary's Church makes a distinct landmark. The date of this aerial shot is uncertain, but at least two features show that it is not a modern one. The area of Baulmesholme, top right, is now obliterated by the giant Carlsberg Brewery. Also, the flood meadows, top left, are now occupied by an extensive trading estate. Development and change are part of a town's organic life, and without them there would be economic stagnation. Northampton has managed to absorb change whilst retaining its essential aspect of a town with plenty of green spaces. The rural is never too far away from the urban in a town which built its reputation on cattle and leather.

Below: The 1960s ushered in the age of the high-rise flats. It seemed a neat enough solution at the time to the problem of housing people relatively cheaply in the face of the spiralling costs of buying building land. Go upwards - New York fashion. The photograph shows the first of the Northampton high-rise flats being erected in The Boroughs, the area of Spring Lane and Scarletwell Street. More were to follow, and even the Mayorhold, an ancient market space in the foreground, was soon to disappear. Nobody at the time was able to forecast the social problems of high-rise living, or how quickly the planners dreams of the 60s would become discredited. To the right of the picture, Grafton Street can be traced upwards and then Spencer Bridge, crossing the railway tracks. If high-rise flats spoke of the future, the railway marshalling yards in the background spoke of the past. The hundreds of goods wagons show how much freight was still carried by British Rail even in the 1960s. This was to go into sad decline with the rise of motorways and the huge expansion of freight transport by road, but who can deny that here too progress has brought its own problems?

On the home front

Above: These hordes of excited wartime children are not digging for victory, but are searching for shrapnel. The occasion was in October 1940 when a returning German bomber jettisoned its remaining bomb on a field in Weston Favell. Northampton got off very lightly in terms of bombing during World War Two compared with nearby Coventry, and that is why the town received so many evacuees. Nevertheless, two incidents occurred which, but for good fortune, could have caused heavy casualties. In January 1941 bombs demolished buildings at St Andrew's Hospital and left huge craters in Billing Road Cemetery. Tombstones crashed through neighbouring roofs, fortunately killing nobody. Rumour had it that gleaming marble tombstones were mistaken by a German bomber for a poorly blacked out munitions factory. Ironically, however, the worst damage of all was done by a British plane, later in the war. A crippled Stirling bomber, abandoned by its crew at night over open land, changed course of its own accord. The empty plane roared dramatically down Gold Street and crashed in George Row. Luckily the bombs did not explode, but the ensuing blaze triggered off machine-gun bullets. The only casualty, however, was a policeman who was blown off his bike and suffered a broken leg.

Left: *During the Second World War, voluntary service by civilians was regarded as extremely important, for the upkeep of morale if nothing else. In May 1940 the government appealed to those who were not in military service to join the Local Defence Volunteers (LDV), renamed the Home Guard in July 1940. Their first task was very specific - to defend strategic and vulnerable points against enemy paratroop attack. Even at the time it was realised that volunteers would be able to do little against highly trained parachutists and jokers were quick to suggest that LDV stood for 'Look, Duck and Vanish'. The initial problem was a shortage of weapons. To drill with walking-sticks became a familiar routine, and early weapons included clubs, spears, air pistols and shotguns. In fact Major General Sir Hereward Wake, in charge of the Northamptonshire Home Guard, was heard to wonder if shotguns were legal under the Geneva Convention! However, even by 1941 training and equipment had much improved, and these smart looking men on the photograph belie the 'Dad's Army' image. They are assembling the 59 parts of their Sten guns in a demonstration before an attentive crowd at Abington Park.*

Below: *Once the Home Guard had become better equipped, the crucial need was for training, and it became compulsory to attend at least 48 hours training per month. There were also major exercises in both town and countryside. The photograph, which shows a bicycle messenger from ARP (Air Raid Precaution) bringing instructions to Home Guard sentries in Bridge Street, was probably part of such an exercise. The concrete blocks stand ready to be rolled into position to form an anti-tank barrier. Some 750 of these were deposited at various strategic points around Northampton; some are still to be found here and there. Another problem of the Home Guard was its age composition. It tended to be made up of those too young for active service in the armed forces and those too old - 'Long Dentured Veterans' was another variation on the LDV theme. The sentries on Bridge Street appear to be on the youthful side, although the one on the left is well-trained enough to be holding his Sten gun in the proper fashion in the circumstances. At the other extreme Thomas Walton of Northampton, aged 84 in 1940, was the oldest Home Guard volunteer in Britain, having knocked 20 years off his age in order to enlist.*

They are trying their best to look brave, but the bewilderment and anxiety on the faces of these evacuees from Ipswich cannot help coming through. The scene is Cedar Road School in 1939 and these children are obviously receiving a warm reception from a kindly receptionist. The prospect of massive casualties from heavy bombing was the great fear of the government on the outbreak of war, and the process of evacuating children from target areas to safer zones had been going on even before the war began. By the end of September, Northamptonshire had absorbed 42,529 evacuees. Northampton itself took around 15,000, many from Ipswich, but amongst them were also some Polish and German refugee children who were given temporary accommodation at Rothersthorpe Road School, Far Cotton. Taking in evacuees was one thing; keeping them was another. Between September 1939 and April 1940, the period known as the phoney war, there were no air-raids to speak of and most children returned to their families.

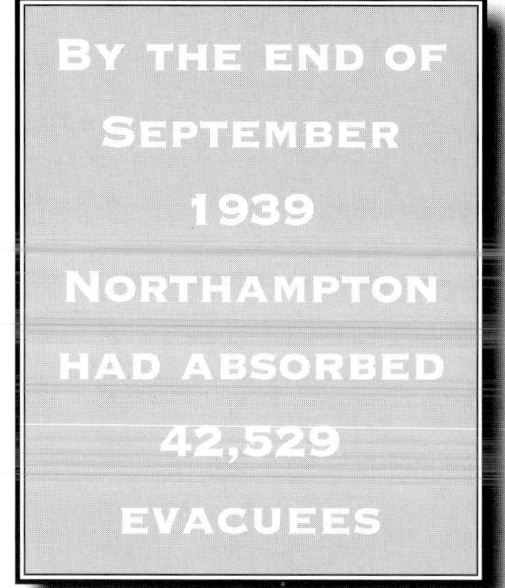

Eighty percent of Northampton's evacuees went back home in this period. However, in September 1940 the Blitz began in earnest, and many evacuees flooded back. Whatever their inner turmoil, the children in the photograph were in a relatively safe area and amongst generous hosts.

At leisure

Above: There is no mistaking Tom Walls, the dapper little gentleman in the middle of the front row. A famous stage and screen star of the 1930s, he is pictured here with the staff of the Exchange Cinema. Tom was born at Byron Street in Northampton and he first achieved fame in the Aldwych farces with Robertson Hare. His great passion other than acting was horses, and he later went to live at the nearby village of Chapel Brampton, from which he was more easily able to follow his beloved Pytchley Hunt. As a great horse-racing enthusiast, he achieved a lifetime ambition when his horse, 'April V', won the Epsom Derby in 1932. Tom's appearance at the Exchange Cinema was on the occasion of the premiere of one of his films, 'The Blarney Stone'. The Exchange had opened in 1920 and was the town's most palatial cinema. What is amazing by modern standards is the number of uniformed staff on the photograph. The bow-tied manager, 'Pat' Thornton, stands on the right, whilst the girl on the far left proudly clutches an autographed programme. The advertisement for Boris Karloff, in 'The Old Dark House', is enough to send shivers down the spine of older readers.

Top: No stern and straight-faced pose for the camera as is so often seen in old photographs. These young ladies offer only friendly smiles as they perambulate along Paradise Walk in 1937. The picture was taken from the bottom of Cheyne Walk, looking towards Bedford Road, and is evocative in so many ways. The railings on the right enclosed land that was then known as Cow Meadow and there may be some senior citizens who remember Frisian cows grazing there. It is, of course now known as Becket's Park. The railings have been removed and the asphalt path replaced by grass. The cooling tower to the right belonged to the Hardingstone Junction Power Station, and was later joined by two others. They have all since been demolished. One intriguing part of this 1937 scene is to see a man pushing a pram - quite unusual for that era. But back to the young ladies. Paradise Walk was clearly a lovely place to stroll and chat whilst taking baby on an outing, and possibly these were nannies. There is just a suggestion, however, that these are not young ladies, but young girls pushing dolls prams. Have a close look. What do you think?

The simple fun and pleasure of drinking at a public fountain seems now to belong to a far-off age. Indeed the dress of the children seems to put this scene back into the 1930s or 1940s, although this type of drinking fountain still had a good few years to run yet. What is most striking about the big boy are his 'long short' trousers and his sturdy boots. But if you can't wear boots in Northampton, then where can you wear them? He is helping with the tap, and those who experienced it will remember the hexagonal shape which gave you enough grip to abruptly turn the fountain of water up. Then the little bubble of water became a jet, and it might be suspected that the little boy is about to feel this up his nose. Of course, for the little girl, the achievement will be for her to get her lips to the water at all. This particular fountain was located in Abington Park, near the wall between the bowling green and the thatched farm outbuilding. They were originally installed as a service to the community, but modern health requirements have seen the fountains banished from our parks forever.

Above: Any moment now there will be a large splash, and probably an excited scream, as the first of the figures on the platform careers down the water chute. This happy summer scene was captured in 1956 at Overstone Solarium, a pleasure park on the outskirts of town. Britain does not have the ideal climate for open-air swimming pools, but on the right day it can be an exhilarating experience to swim or just splash about - all in the glorious fresh air. On the other hand, you can choose just to laze around and watch. The line of spectators behind the roof ridge have certainly got a 'bird's eye view.' Whether idly spectating or taking to the water, people are relaxing and enjoying themselves. Swimming has grown in popularity since the growth of municipal baths in the nineteenth century. These were designed partly for recreation, and partly to deter people from swimming in rivers, canals and dams, with all the attendant risks to health and safety. The pool at Overstone Solarium was a very fine one, but its future fate can be glimpsed at top right. The pleasure park became a caravan site, with the pool sliced in half to leave a small paddling pool.

Below: Little Tony Forward's career was mapped out almost from the start and here he is at the tender age of four, learning to cope with the media. Tony, a Northampton boy, was the son of Alan Forward (pictured on the left) who was a successful grass track racer. Tony became the mascot of the Brandon Bees speedway team, and he led them around on their parade laps. This is where it might have ended, for child mascots in all sports tend to disappear into their different walks of life at a later stage.
However, motor-cycle racing was in Tony's blood, and he went on to ride the Continental circuit as a professional speedway and grass track racer with great success. Speedway racing has had bouts of great popularity since the war and it can certainly provide an exciting spectacle. A first time visitor is usually amazed by the sheer noise as the bikes open up and jostle for position on the first bend, or is intrigued by that distinctive smell of high octane fuel hanging in the air. Tony became 'hooked' by the thrills and spills, and from watching his heroes he went on to become a big name himself.

Above: A sight to inspire terror in the stoutest defence as a close formation of footballing fillies approaches, using not just one ball but two! Girls' football teams are quite common today, but it was once a novelty to see the 'fairer sex' in soccer kit. These were, in fact, chorus girls from the New Theatre who had come to the County Ground and donned the colours of the 'Cobblers' for a publicity shot. The eye-catching and unusual picture then appeared in the 'Chronicle and Echo' as an inducement to Northamptonians to 'Come to the Show,' for indeed that was what the show was called. The New Theatre closed its doors for ever in 1958 and the photograph seems to date from the earlier part of that decade. The baggy shorts and collared shirts point to that time, along with leather footballs that turned to 'puddings' in wet weather. It would be interesting to know if this publicity stunt had any success, for overall the New Theatre went into steady decline in the post-war years. More intriguingly, did the players of Northampton Town ever appear as 'chorus girls' at the New Theatre in order to boost gates?

Above right: Scenes of unrestrained joy greet the photographer in the Northampton dressing room as an historic occasion is celebrated. By securing a 1-1 draw at home with Portsmouth, in front of an ecstatic crowd of 20,660, the 'Cobblers' had attained First Division status for the first time in their history. Despite the humble beer crate on the table, it's the champagne corks that are popping. Devoted football fans watch their little dramas played out on the pitch and soon come to accept that this week's joy could be next week's despair. Followers of the 'Cobblers,' however, between 1958 and 1970 saw drama on an epic scale, and the ultimate feeling may well have been one of disbelief. Between 1958 and 1965 Northampton Football Club made an extraordinary surge through four divisions to find itself playing alongside football's elite. By August 1965, under skipper Theo Foley, the 'Cobblers' were kicking off against Everton in their first ever top division match. Unfortunately the club was relegated at the end of that season, and again the following season. By 1970 the 'Cobblers' were back in the Fourth Division. The only possible consolation to travelling fans was that it gave them the chance to visit every Football League ground in the country!

It's 1932 and one of the hottest heat-waves for years. The little boy is dressed for the occasion in the height of swimsuit fashion, but he has sensibly kept his footwear on. No doubt the road was burning hot under his feet. Protection against the sun was pretty rudimentary is those far-off days. Nobody had even heard of thinning ozone layers and dangerous ultra-violet rays. As for high factor sun cream ... well, a dab of calamine lotion if you were lucky, usually after the damage had been done! It's not clear what the policeman is doing. He may be stopping the traffic (which seems to be non-existent); or he may be sending the lad home to put something respectable on; or he may be pointing the way to the nearest paddling pool. One thing is for certain, he will have to sweat it out in his blue serge uniform. No walking about in shirt sleeves for bobbies in those days! Long, hot summers are the stuff of childhood memories, along with sticky fly papers hanging from the ceiling if you go back far enough. But let's not forget that the year of the drought was only back in 1995.

A wealth of history at the heart of Northampton

The early years

Church's China, one of Northampton's longest established retail businesses has been a central feature of Northampton business for over 120 years. For most of those years the company has been situated in the town's huge and impressive Market Square, generally recognised as one of the largest in Great Britain. If a family business could write history, Church's China could uniquely claim to have observed the passing of more than a century of life outside its doors; violent demonstrations, military parades, numerous royal visits, carnivals, circuses and parades. From quaint Victorian bonnets to punk headgear. From penny farthings to Porsches. All this and so much more has come and gone - all quietly witnessed by a family China shop.

> In that old Potter's Shop I stand alone,
> With the clay population round in rows,
> And strange to tell among that earthen lot,
> Some could articulate while others not;
> And suddenly one more important cried -
> Who is the Potter, pray, and who is the Pot?
>
> *Omar Khyyam*

Above:*Wesley Church, who with his father, founded the company.* ***Below:*** *Parade House - the company's first home in Northampton.*

Church's China was founded in the middle of the nineteenth century. Thomas Church, who had been a wheelwright and joiner, set up the company in 1858, taking over the premises at 16 Maryport Street, Devizes. Thomas was aided in his venture by his son, Wesley, who, in the early 1870s, brought the business to Northampton. Wesley soon married Sarah Spencer, from a Northampton family of shoemakers. They set up home and shop in Parade House, a former hotel on the north face of Northampton's Market Square; the site is currently occupied by Boots.

Soon after moving to Northampton, Church's were unwittingly involved in violent scenes of political unrest. The year was 1874.

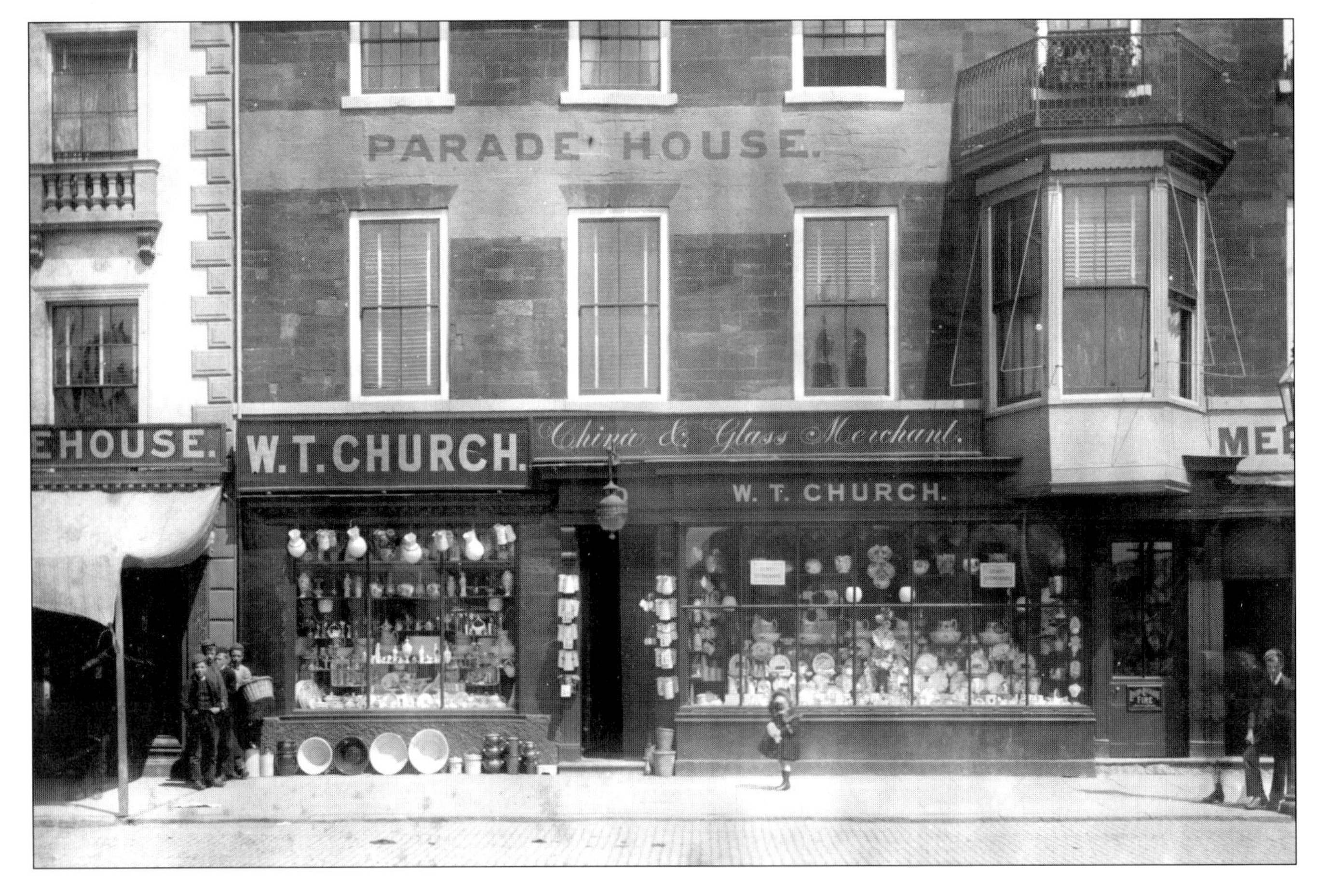

A Westminster by-election was held in the town and Charles Bradlaugh won the seat for the Liberal Party. A renowned atheist and radical, Bradlaugh was not allowed to take oath on the Bible in the House of Commons. Consequently, his election was declared void and a second vote was held. He won again, and fearing that their man was once more to be refused entry into parliament, the locals rioted in the Market Square, smashing windows of both the newspaper offices and the china shop next door. It was only on the arrival of the local militia that the crowd dispersed.

It was in Parade House in 1882 that Wilfrid Church, the third generation member of the business, was born. Years later, Wilfrid described, in his memoirs, life on the market square at the end of the century:

LOCALS RIOTED IN THE MARKET SQUARE, SMASHING WINDOWS OF BOTH THE NEWSPAPER OFFICES AND THE CHINA SHOP

"The rooms in these old premises were large and spread out. The different floors were approached by a balustraded and wide staircase which reached up to the top storey. The ground levels were occupied by the showrooms and general stock, except for a capacious kitchen and a terrifying 'coal hole.' This culinary department was stone flagged and was a happy playground for cockroaches. The beetle trap was constantly in requisition and a kettle of boiling water was served out to them in the mornings. At the rear of the building was a patch of pasture on which a Mr Ambridge, a butcher, would graze a few sheep, which were evidently en route for slaughter."

Next to Parade House were the offices and printing presses of the Northampton Mercury (now the Mercury & Herald). Wilfrid and his friends would prowl amongst the heaps of obsolete machinery and collect odd bits of type discarded by the setters. Much to his mother's annoyance he would slope back home, his clothes covered in printing ink.

In those days the market square was full of life and bustle, and not just with the daily activity of the market stalls. Wilfrid remembered the arrival of the fair with "round-a-bouts, boxing booths and snapdragon confections. The glare and tumult persisted until about 11.00pm when the bellowing organ gave as its lullaby, 'Christians Awake'.

"About the first week in June, wagons of wool would arrive drawn by sturdy horses. These were from the outlying farms and soon unloaded,

Top: *The Bradlaugh Riots which took place in 1874. Church's shop was dragged into the row when its windows were smashed.*

W. T. CHURCH
7, Sheep St.
Is now selling, for a short time only, previous to Stock-taking. ::
Goods at about HALF PRICE

Bargains in China & Glass.

Now is your chance for getting a High-class China Limoges Dinner Set £7 7s. for £4 19s., or a Minton 70-piece Dinner Set £2 12s. for 35s. Royal Worcester Tea Sets, 40 pieces.
Oddments 10 to 50 per cent. below cost

W. T. Church, 7, SHEEP ST

weighed and bid for. The Cheese Fair was also an attraction, when the large cylindrical blocks were brought for sale from many parts. A gauge-like knife could be inserted for the prospective buyer to judge whether the commodity was to his taste or not. On one occasion a menagerie arrived on the square, the roar of wild beasts sounding somewhat fearsome during the night."

Being the focal point of the town, there was always plenty going on. Wilfrid remembered politicians holding forth from the steps of the fountain. They were sometimes "baptised by little urchins who had climbed up above and flipped water from the ornamental cupolas". Wilfrid also had vivid memories of the noisy activity of the printing presses in the newspaper offices next door, and how when the editions of the 'Mercury' were released, there would be a stampede of newspaper boys along the passageway adjoining the shop. The hordes of youths would pour out in all directions across the Market Square. "As the partition was flimsy, the vases and ornaments would jump up and down and rattle as though in an earthquake."

Business progressed quietly and unremarkably. Of the few activities that stand out in Wilfrid's mind was the annual 'packing' at Castle Ashby. He recalls one such occasion when as a boy of nine, he accompanied his father to the stately home.

"At a certain time of year the Marquis of Northampton would visit Exmoor on a stag hunting expedition, taking with him a fairly large retinue. At such times, my father would be requisitioned to visit Castle Ashby to pack up china and glass for their safe conveyance to the hunting grounds. There in the large servants' hall in the castle, I can remember joining in the lunch with the large number of servants and general staff, the baker, the butler, the housekeeper and the coachman. After this repast, I was taken across a snow covered park to see Knuckle Bone Arbour, a bower or retreat, the floor of which was laid with the knuckle bones of deer."

The Emporium Arcade
At the end of the century, the Church family were shattered to hear that their shop was to be demolished to make way for a modern development known as 'The Arcade Emporium'. They moved the business to No. 7 Sheep Street. In those days, as today, position was all important, and situated on the wrong side of a busy and dangerous thoroughfare, trade suffered. Perhaps the bargains offered in this advert are hints of the tough times of this period (top).

EXCEPTIONAL SELECTION OF DINNER SETS, TEA SETS, & TOILET SETS
Worcester, Wedgwood, Royal Crown Derby China, &c.
11 The Parade, (MARKET SQUARE) Northampton,
Dr. to CHURCH & SON
(ESTABLISHED NEARLY 70 YEARS)
China, Glass & Earthenware Dealers
Country Orders Punctually Dispatched
GOODS ON HIRE

Wilfrid Church, now a young businessman in his late twenties, was keen to revive the fortunes of the family concern and arranged a return to the Market Square. On June 26th 1911, Church's China moved back to its original position on Northampton's Market Square, this time at the front of a splendid new Shopping Arcade.

This picture (facing page, bottom) is an architect's watercolour of the Emporium Arcade. Although it is architecturally accurate, there never was a Wedgwood shop to the left of the entrance. A contemporary description accompanying the watercolour states: "The building extends over 300 feet from front to back and contains upwards of 50 shops, several suites of offices, a gymnasium hall, several meeting rooms, a basement cafe, a restaurant approached directly from the Market Square, a hairdresser's salon and public conveniences. The building is lit throughout by electricity. The entrance archway is decorated with white, green and purple Doulton tiles."

The Market Square was still the very heart of Northampton life. On occasions, daily life would be enhanced by the visit of the circus. This wonderful old photograph catches the delightful moment when a stallholder's wares are consumed by a trio of hungry elephants (below).

Advertisements were now becoming more sophisticated. This example (top) from 1924 gives a rare insight into the interior of the premises.
This bill (above) offers a suggestion of the kind of goods on offer some eighty years ago. As well as tea cups and saucers, Church's sold such obscure artefacts as slop basins.

Above: *Wilfrid Church, Wesley's son.*

For over sixty years, Church's China occupied the front of the Emporium Arcade. During this period, trade, whilst not exciting, was sufficient to keep the Church family comfortably off. Between the two World Wars, Wilfrid and his wife Naomi raised four children, the youngest of whom, Vivian, joined the business in 1954. The war years were naturally difficult. Money was short and trade suffered. During the Second World War, Wilfrid 'did his bit' as part of the local Air Raid Protection unit. In this capacity, he spent many a long night at the shop 'keeping watch'. To make the time pass, he used his considerable skills of craftsmanship to construct display shelving out of old tea chests. Today, such thrifty ingenuity would doubtless earn him an environmental award!

DURING THE WAR WILFRID USED HIS SKILLS TO CONSTRUCT DISPLAY SHELVING OUT OF OLD TEA CHESTS

Crucial to the success of the business from the early 1950s until his retirement in 1992 was the manager, Peter Andrews. Peter began with Church's after serving in the R.A.F. and spending a brief time in the leather trade. He soon developed a deep knowledge of the product and a tremendous gift for getting on with customers. Peter had a tremendous ability to get inside the minds of Church's customers, and had the invariable knack of knowing what they wanted before they even knew it themselves. He was instrumental in building up the prosperous 'customer base' that sustained Church's during the post war period.

In 1965, Wilfrid's son Vivian, now heading the business, took the bold step of taking on the other side of the front of the Arcade. This gave the business an imposing frontage, and several thousand square feet of showrooms on three floors.

The shop featured a very early Express lift. Vivian's sons Philip, Richard and Stephen, today all involved in the business, have vivid memories of the clanking old lift, with its 'concertina' iron gates, a potentially lethal trap for idly wandering fingers. It is extraordinary to think in these days when customer access is so important to retail success, and when Fire Regulations are so strict, that with no staircase, the sole means of passage between floors was in a rickety old lift.

Although Wilfrid Church was an astute though (of necessity) a cautious businessman, he preferred to stay in the background, carrying out his office duties. Vivian, however, having inherited his mother's outgoing temperament, has played an altogether different role in the business. Vivian was (and still is!) masterful at employing his tremendous sense of humour in selling to customers. There are literally hundreds who can vividly recall him demonstrating the strength of fine bone china by hurling plates to the floor or pirouetting on upturned tea cups. Vivian has also been innovative in his business planning. In his design of the Emporium Arcade expansion in the mid-sixties and the move into Welsh House in the seventies, he showed tremendous imagination. Furthermore, his concept of developing a cookshop side to the business in 1965 was years ahead of its time. Customer care has always been a funda-

mental consideration. To this end, his introduction of free gift wrapping (hitherto unheard of) was a major innovation.

In the early 1970s, in an almost eerie repetition of what had occurred at the turn of the century, Church's China were informed that they had to vacate their position on the Market Square. Again, they were forced to make way for a new shopping development, and again they took temporary refuge in Sheep Street. In fact, during this second period of exile from the Market Square, Church's occupied two shops; one in Sheep Street in a converted garage

Above: *The Emporium Arcade - the company's home for over 60 years.*

showroom currently occupied by Durham Pine. The other shop was at the top of the Drapery from where Thomas Cook now operate.

As the photo above illustrates, the Sheep Street premises were perhaps a little spartan, but business, along with the economy of Northampton as a whole, was booming.

1975 witnessed another exciting move for Church's, as for the third time in 105 years the business took occupancy in Northampton's Market Square. The town centre had developed beyond all recognition; the entire area known as Newland had been replaced by an extensive two storey shopping mall, the Grosvenor Centre. The Market Square entrance to the centre was overlooked by the recently restored Jacobean frontage of Welsh House. The building has a colourful history. It was built towards the end of the sixteenth century for a firm of lawyers, and in 1675 featured in the Great Fire of Northampton. The town centre was destroyed and one of the few escape routes for the inhabitants of the Market Square was through Welsh House into the fields beyond.

Welsh House stands as a reminder of Northampton's historic links with Wales. There is more than one theory as to the origin of the name, Welsh House. One is that the firm of lawyers for whom it was built were of Gaellic extraction. An alternative idea is more agricultural. In the sixteenth century, Welsh drovers would herd sheep, cattle and even geese down the old Roman road of Watling Street (the A5), to sell them on Northampton's Market Square. On occasions, these drovers would stay overnight in the building. Whatever the reason for its name, the Welsh link is indisputable, for even today, if you look at the crests on the front of the building, you will see the Welsh Dragon, the crest of Llewelyn, Prince of Wales and the Welsh Motto "Heb Dyw Heb Dim, Dyw y Digon" (Without God Without Anything, God is Enough).

One of the key roles played by Welsh House was that, for many years in the eighteenth century, it housed the original offices of the Northampton Mercury (now part of the Chronicle & Echo). This newspaper proudly holds the record of the longest surviving provincial newspaper in Britain.

Above: *Sheep Street in the 1970s.*

premises in St Giles Street. Formerly Stantons the stationers and printers, the new 3,500 square foot store was opened in August of that year by Lord Wedgwood.

The next 140 years

There has been so much change since the humble beginnings of 1858. Generations have come and gone. Trends in product range have ever shifted. Chamber pots and water sets have been replaced by sculpted resin Cottages and Irish Coffee glasses. The clientele has changed. 'Old money' or the 'County Set' have been replaced by a much broader customer base, encompassing all parts of the local community. Immaculately hand-written double-entry book-keeping procedures have been superseded by computerised accounts, spreadsheets and databases. But none of this really matters. At Church's China, what still counts are traditional human values - the provision of the very finest in gifts, tableware and housewares along with a commitment to service with a sense of fun.

Church's not only occupied three floors of Welsh House, but had also taken a unit on the first floor of the Grosvenor Centre, offering the unique opportunity to present alternative faces to the buying public; one a contemporary, modern feel, the other a more traditional appeal. Both departments enjoyed success and in the the 1980s, with Vivian's sons Philip, Richard and Stephen in the business, a period of expansion ensued, with branches opening in Banbury, Rugby, Kettering and Peterborough. Then in 1996, with the Welsh House lease coming to an end, the opportunity arose to take up new

Above: *Welsh House.*
Below: *The St Giles Street premises, opened in August 1996 by Lord Wedgwood.*

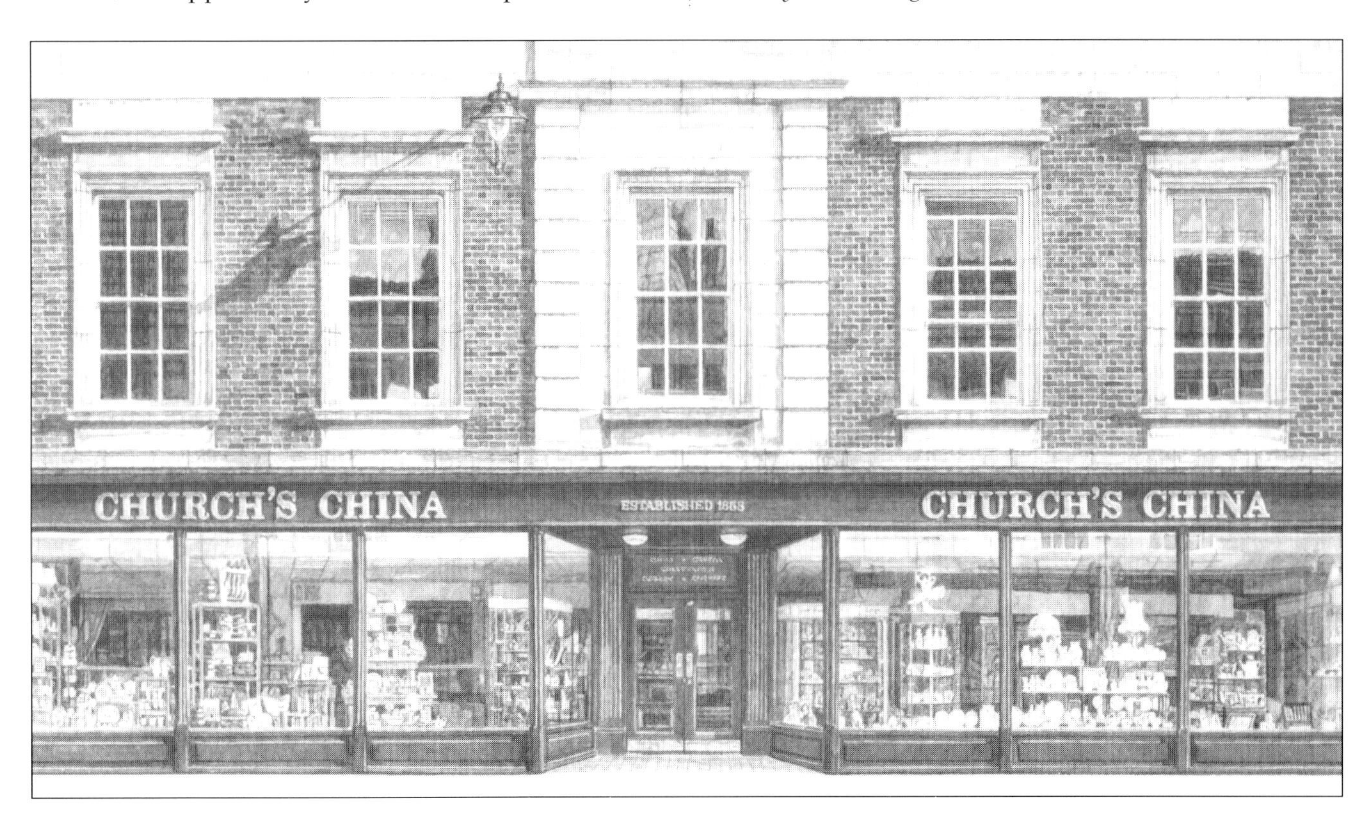

Events & occasions

Left: May 12th 1937 marked the Coronation of King George VI and Queen Elizabeth. In common with the rest of the country, Northampton celebrated the occasion with rejoicing and patriotic fervour. People were glad of a joyous royal event which might relieve the general gloom of national and international affairs at that time. Only the year before, in 1936, the abdication crisis concerning King Edward VIII's association with the American divorcee, Mrs Wallis Simpson, had caused constitutional problems. Abroad, Hitler had begun his aggressive moves and was now allied to the Italian dictator, Mussolini. If people needed a chance to forget all this, albeit briefly, then the 1937 Coronation provided it. Northampton streets were lavishly decorated for the great day and this photograph shows The Drapery. Shops and public buildings are hung with giant flags, and streamers criss-cross the street. Apart from the vehicles, the two ladies' cloche hats on view give the scene a 1930s feel, as does the old light standard in the middle of the road. A shopper looking at the same scene now would probably be focusing on Debenhams, half-way down the right-hand side of The Drapery where, in 1937, Adnitt's store stood.

Above: Tremendous efforts were made to bring colour and pageantry into the streets of Northampton in May 1937, and the local council did a fine job in having several triumphal arches erected in the town centre. This wonderful effort was to be found on Abington Street. It manages to combine a patriotic and loyal message with a neat reference to Northampton's traditional involvement in leather and shoes. More decorations are visible further along the street and even the barrels housing the temporary erecting posts have been given fancy wrappings. The rather impressive building housing the Northampton Town and County Building Society, far right, is plentifully adorned with streamers, emblems and flags, and there is no doubt that the colours red, white and blue will have been predominant. This building now houses BBC Radio Northampton.

Abington Street itself looks fairly quiet for a Coronation day, with cyclists outnumbering cars. However, it is probable that the photographer was out-and-about early, in order to get his shots before the streets became too congested. Also, in the 1930s, maybe the cyclists always outnumbered the cars in Northampton!

The newly constructed All Saints Parish Hall, on Horseshoe Street is absolutely packed for a Coronation celebration tea on May 12th 1937. There seems to be not an inch to spare as the guests pause a moment for the photographer before falling on the sandwiches, buns and fizzy drinks. It is an occasion that is clearly meant for children in the main, although not entirely so. Some patriotic hats are on display and from the clothing worn by some of the children, there is just a suggestion that a fancy dress parade has been incorporated into the day's events. At the rear of the hall, distinguished visitors look on benignly and no doubt they will be nibbling at a little something themselves. It is interesting to speculate what state those beautifully clean table-cloths were in by the end of the afternoon. The line of helpers standing along the left-hand wall, many of them in 'pinnies', had no doubt slaved for hours to prepare this feast. And, even on Coronation Day, somebody has to do the washing up. Imagine what that would amount to in an age where there were no such things as disposable plastic plates and cups!

Below: Plenty of smiles for the camera outside All Saints Parish Hall on that Coronation Day of over 60 years ago. Most of these youngsters will now be senior citizens, but there might still be one or two copies of this photograph tucked away in albums somewhere, a treasured memory. Keen-eyed readers might be able to identify some of the faces here in the other photograph concerning All Saints. Plenty of imagination has gone into the fancy dress, with probably the most light-weight jockey of all time on the front row. The patriotically decorated bike too deserves to have won a prize. Scenes like this were repeated across Northampton as scores of streets and roads hung up their decorations and celebrated the Coronation. Games, sports, teas, music, dancing, motor bus tours of the town centre decorations - these were the recurrent themes. There were, however, more unusual aspects. On St David's Road there was an 'ankle competition'. All the children of Vicarage Lane, Kingsthorpe, had a TSB account opened for them. Younger children on Dallington Road received a Coronation mug, filled with chocolates, whilst older boys received an engraved pocket knife, and girls an inscribed compact. Most mysterious of all, Wantage Road held a 'smoking competition!'

Bottom: This view of St Giles Street on Coronation Day 1937 just takes in the corner of the Town Hall, on the left, showing to good effect some of the fine carvings on this building. To the right, the substantial and solid edifice of the Prudential Building houses its own offices and the premises of Montagu Jeffrey underneath. Once again streamers and flags are to the fore as the street prepares itself for the events of the day ahead. Perhaps the policeman cycling his way up the street in the distance was on his way to his duty point for the Grand Parade. The latter was one of the major events of Northampton's celebrations of May 12th and it involved 50 decorated lorries in a procession that was nearly one mile long. It was led by the Syncopated Players' Band, closely followed by the Shoe Trade Queen, Miss Winifred Bull, surrounded by Union Jacks. The lorries that followed each carried a tableau depicting an episode in the history of Northampton, or a depiction of the town's life and work. All this was staged by Northampton schoolchildren who had rehearsed and worked for weeks in preparation for the event.

The shadows across Bridge Street give an indication that Coronation Day 1937 turned out to be a sunny one. No doubt the sunshine enhanced the patriotic colours on the streamers and flags. A BSA motorbike with delivery sidecar is parked in a rough and ready fashion at the right-hand side of the street. Lee's tobacconists, on the far right, proudly advertises its 'Superb Abdullah Cigarettes', whilst lower down the sign for 'Foyles 2d Library' gives some idea of the humble beginnings of this now large organisation. The man leaning on the belisha beacon seems to have no intention of crossing the road.

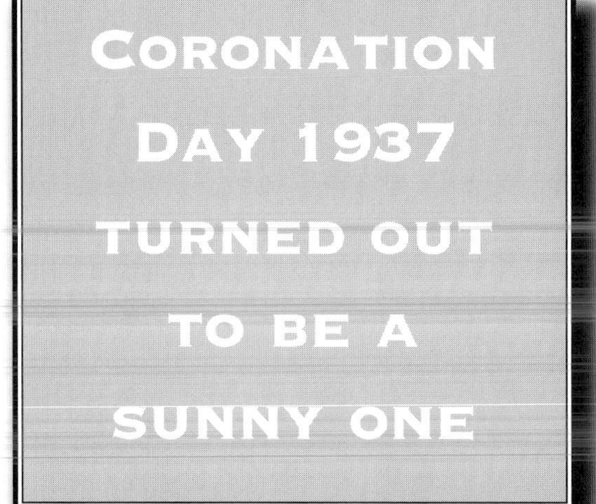

Many shots of the 1930s feature working men in regulation flathats and mufflers in a 'nothing to do, nowhere to go' pose. Perhaps this one is simply staking his claim early for a good view of the Grand Parade. In which case he will have been treated to dozens of tableaux including, 'Homage to Learning' by the girls of Northampton School, clad in Greek robes; the 'Trial of Thomas a Becket at Northampton Castle,' by Spencer School; or even, the 'English Gypsies Salute Their King' by the Roadmender Boys' Club.

Above: Princess Elizabeth, with Earl Spencer just to the rear, proceeds down an aisle of nurses on her departure from Northampton General Hospital. July 30th 1946 was a 'red letter' day for the town, marking as it did Princess Elizabeth's first official visit. A spot of royal pageantry and colour was an ideal morale booster in these grim post-war years, with rationing and shortages still blighting the country. The visit, however, had a definite purpose. In 1944 the hospital war appeal for £250,000 had been launched, with each town and village in the area allotted a target. The Princess was visiting the hospital to award souvenir cards to the delegates of 103 places which had exceeded their targets. Huge, enthusiastic crowds greeted the royal car as it made its way from the borough boundary to the General Hospital. Flag-waving schoolchildren cheered at the tops of their voices, and the corner of Cheyne Walk and St Giles Street found people perched on window sills and even roofs. Before touring the hospital, Princess Elizabeth presented the token cards. Each one outlined the nature of the award, accompanied by the phrase, 'Sweet mercy is nobility's true badge'.

Top: On leaving the nurses' home at the General Hospital, the Princess made the short walk to the childrens' ward and the Barratt Maternity Home. Having left the formality of the presentation behind, it was during this part of the visit that the happiest and most touching scenes of the day were enacted. The Princess met children whose ages ranged from five days to nine years, and children are nothing if not spontaneous. Outside the children's ward, in the warm sunshine, she chatted with 14 children surrounded by their toys. She seemed delighted by their responses, not least by the fact that two of them slept soundly, blissfully unaware of the royal presence. She was obviously moved, however, by the plight of some of the sick children. Princess Elizabeth then went on to mingle with the mothers and expectant mothers in the Maternity Home. The latter was presented to Northampton by Mr W Barratt, the prominent shoe manufacturer. Hence, 'to walk the Barratt way' in Northampton, means to be pregnant. It is doubtful if anyone informed the Princess of this! The photograph shows her inspecting an ATS guard of honour on her departure. The Princess herself had served with the ATS during the war.

Below: There was something definitely afoot on the wide spaces of Abington Street in June 1953. A fairly quiet time of day has been chosen for putting the final touches to the decorations, or perhaps it was even the morning of the great day itself - June 2nd 1953. A feeling of barely suppressed excitement lay beneath the calm for this day was a landmark, the Coronation of Queen Elizabeth II, the dawn of the new Elizabethan Age. It was time at last to shake off the drab years of post-war austerity. The centre of Northampton became a sea of colour - mainly red, white and blue -as shops and public buildings were festooned with flags, emblems, bunting and streamers. Huge banners and emblematic crowns were the theme of Abington Street, although a massive Union Jack has been unfurled from the roof of the rather splendid looking Notre Dame Convent and School, to the right. Elsewhere in the town centre the story was much the same as the people of Northampton set out to show that, in terms of patriotism, they were second to none.

Right: Over in Market Square, at the offices of the 'Chronicle and Echo,' a more than lifesize portrait of the new Queen is being carefully put into position. The crowning of a young queen captured everybody's imagination and the atmosphere was full of new found optimism. The Coronation of 1953 was the first real national celebration since VE Day in 1945. Even that had been tinged by anxiety and sadness for some, and had been followed by continued years of shortages and rationing. Nineteen fifty three marked a psychological moment in terms of letting go of the past and a turning towards the future. The portrait on the front of the newspaper offices is so striking that Northamptonians who were living at the time will surely remember it. If not that, something of that unforgettable day will have impressed itself on the mind. The operation looks to be quite a tricky one as workmen cling to ladders and hang out of windows. One thing is for sure, the Coronation provided plenty of overtime for those in the building trades.

Long Live The
KEEP
LEFT

Below: A wonderful splash of colour must have greeted the photographer's eye as he captured this scene in the closing room of J Sears & Co, shoe manufacturers. Wherever the people of Northampton came together to work - shops, mills, schools, hospitals - imaginative minds and busy hands produced decorations that were fit for a new monarch and a new era. The ladies at Sears (and a few men) are in party mood judging by their cheerful faces and the amount of 'liquid refreshment' on the go. They earned their break too considering the amount of effort that must have gone into the superb decorations. As they were hanging the streamers they may well have been humming along to the big 'hit' melody of the time, 'Elizabethan Serenade.' Many may remember that evocative piece of music, which seemed to be on the radio every two minutes. It is difficult to imagine that those sewing machines ever really got cracking again that day, or that those piles of leather got much smaller!

Left: The workman sums up his options as he stands, fairly securely, on the roof above the entrance to the ABC Cinema. He almost appears to be consulting the portrait of Prince Philip as to where to place the roundels of the young children, Charles and Anne. The Queen's family were not forgotten in the 1953 Coronation celebrations, for this was part of the appeal, a young couple with a young family. People could identify with this. Youth was increasingly to come to the fore in the 1950s and the launching of a new magazine, 'The Young Elizabethan,' seemed to capture the mood of it all. Once the portraits were erected, passers-by enjoyed a good view from the street below, and an even better one from the top deck of a bus, of a happy family scene. Young royals are ever popular, no matter how troubled the affairs of the monarchy might be, and they often set a fashion in names. And so, any readers of late 1940s or early 1950s vintage, named Charles or Anne, might put two and two together.

Above: When the much awaited day of June 2nd 1953 at last arrived, the British weather naturally rose to the occasion. It was generally dull and cold, with squally bursts of rain. Nevertheless the people of Northampton were determined to enjoy themselves and the weather did not prevent an eruption of street parties which had been planned for months. The photographer has caught an absolute sea of colour along Gladstone Terrace in a scene that was so typical of the day. Most of the celebrations took place in the afternoon as everyone wanted to watch the Coronation ceremony on television around midday. In 1953, of course, televisions were quite a rarity and there was a good deal of communal viewing of televisions set up in school and church halls. The screens were small; the images were black-and-white and of poor quality; but anyone who watched that day will not have forgotten the experience. Then it was off to the street parties! The children of Gladstone Terrace are obviously enjoying themselves. There are plenty of caps and short pants in evidence, for there was no pressure for children to look 'cool'

Top: The importance of the occasion cannot be lost on these children of Stimpson Avenue School as they collect their Coronation souvenirs in June 1953. Some trouble has been gone to in the erecting of a little dais and in the draping of Union Jacks to form a patriotic backcloth. The sight of that highly polished chair on the dais might evoke an instant recollection of school days to some. That style of teacher's chair, once so common in schools, is quite a rarity in the classroom now. The ceremony of the occasion is an indication of just how loyal the country was to the institution of monarchy in 1953. There was no hint of modern day cynicism in ordinary people's attitudes towards the Crown. It would be surprising if these children had not sung the National Anthem at the end of the presentation, for it was played as a matter of course at all public performances. Not only this, people invariably stood up respectfully. Most probably there was a Coronation mug in the box that the little girl is clutching so earnestly. How many readers got one? How many have still got it?

What a splendid effort was made by the residents of Manor Road, Kingsthorpe, in their fancy-dress parade to celebrate the 1953 Coronation. The little jockey at the front, to the right, is dressed in honour of the great horseracing hero of the day, Gordon Richards. A jockey of a different kind can be seen on the left as the little sheriff 'rides into the sunset' on his wooden horse. Adults and children alike have entered into the spirit of it all. Similar scenes were enacted in countless Northampton streets on that memorable day. Huge quantities of ice-cream and jelly were consumed; souvenir presents were distributed; there were games, races, competitions and treasure hunts. Gwyn Hughes, a wing-half for the 'Cobblers' opened the festivities at Danefield Road, whilst at Gloucester Street Close they were celebrating the winning of the best-decorated street competition. The rain had its way later in the day when the evening fireworks display and decorated boat procession at Becket's Park had to be postponed. Nevertheless the local firemen did not allow the weather to disrupt their display of water jets illuminated by coloured spotlights.

MANOR
RD.
E.R.II.
PHIPPS
ALES &
STOUT.
GOVERMENT
8/-
TWINKLE
TWINKLE
LITTLE
STAR

Above: The Second World War disturbed all sorts of things, in this case the celebrations for the four hundredth anniversary of the founding of Northampton Town and County Grammar School. The school having been founded by Thomas Chipsey in 1541, this important commemoration should have taken place in 1941, but the war put paid to that. Instead it was held in 1947, and the photograph shows Air Chief Marshal Sir Philip Joubert unveiling a plaque over the main entrance to mark the occasion. The school, now the Northampton School for Boys, had interesting origins. It was established in 1541 in what had been St Gregory's Church. This old church had contained a shrine known as the 'rood in the wall.' Here, long ago, a vision of an angel had appeared and declared Northampton to be the centre of England. Whether this had any influence on generations of Geography teachers at the school is not known. The ceremony pictured gives every appearance of having been a splendid occasion. The link with the air-force is clear from the lines of smart air cadets standing at ease. Proud parents look on, and the shorts and pumps on display seem to indicate that a Sports Day will follow.

Above right: The strains of Roll Out the Barrel, hugely popular with the troops during World War Two, will be forever associated with the vivacious Bertha Willmott, pictured here with her husband, Reg Seymour. Bertha's roots were in London. She was born in East Ham, in 1895, and her singing talent was encouraged by the nuns at the convent school she attended. Having begun her stage career in 1912 as Little Mollie, she reverted to her own name in 1914. Radio was to become Bertha's forte and she began to make a name for herself in such programmes as Henry Hall's Guest Night. Northampton first saw this rising star in 1932 when she appeared at the New Theatre in Ridgeway Parade with Ben Warris (although she had appeared earlier in her career as a singer at Rushden Working Men's Club for a fee of £1 15 shillings!). Something about Northampton and its people appealed to Bertha, for in 1938 she and Reg took over the Spinney Hill Hotel. Bertha's career reached its peak during the war when, as part of ENSA, she helped to entertain troops on the radio programme Your Cup of Tea. In her later years she was involved in the campaign to try and save the New Theatre. Her death came in 1978.

Below: Flames shoot through the roof and a huge pall of smoke fills the sky. This dramatic scene was captured some 40 years ago, in September 1959, as the Wright Bros warehouse on the Mounts was consumed by one of the fiercest fires seen in Northampton for many years. The firemen struggled desperately, but the smoke does not quite obscure the notice towards the top of the warehouse indicating that huge stocks of furniture were housed within. Hence the fierceness of the blaze. To make matters worse, the firm next door, Edward C Cook, was a supplier of chemicals for leather, amongst other things. At least there were no people to be rescued, but somebody must have been concerned about the rather fine car seemingly trapped in the compound. Spectacular fires always attract spectators, but it would have been positively dangerous to get too close to this one. The tremendous heat caused the brickwork of St Mary's RC School, to the right, to flake and crumble. Close scrutiny of the photograph will show that the tarmacadam in front of the fire engine is actually burning. As for the photographer himself, he came away from all this with singed eyebrows!

Bottom: Something was certainly afoot in Market Square on the morning of July 9th 1965, and the sight of so many uniforms might suggest a crisis. However, the army and police were not there to quell civil disorder in the streets of Northampton. Further examination of the photograph reveals bandsmen, nurses and boy scouts. All these uniformed groups had been brought in by bus and van to play their part in what was to be a very happy occasion - the visit of Queen Elizabeth II and the Duke of Edinburgh to the town. The maroon Rolls Royce crossed the borough boundary at Weston Favell for the Queen's first visit to Northampton as a reigning monarch. Hundreds of flag-waving and cheering children made sure that she received a very special welcome. The crowds were extremely dense towards the town centre, some people having gained vantage points at top floor windows, or even on roof tops. 'Doesn't she look lovely,' was the cry as the Queen, in a lemon outfit, stepped out of the Rolls Royce at the Guildhall. Here the royal couple were entertained to lunch by the Mayor and Mayoress, Councillor and Mrs Don Wilson, before proceeding on their way, once more to great displays of enthusiasm.

It looks as if the organisers managed to get a fine day for the Carnival Parade of 1955. These are always tremendously popular with young and old alike and an enthusiastic crowd lines the streets. As the Carnival Queen passes the Town Hall she is the focus of attention, but no doubt onlookers were appreciative of the floats that would be following on, not least the amount of work that always goes into them. A prize view has been gained by the people at the windows above the Corner House. The Carnival Queen and her retinue sit in state before a historical backdrop, with the town motto above - 'Castello Fortior Concordia'.

Following on is a 'miniature' queen in a tiny float which seems to be one mass of flowers. A collector in a 'bunny' outfit is shaking her tin, and as the coins begin to fly the boy at the back stoops to make sure none are missed. The Northampton Carnival began as a Cycle Parade in 1890 and still lives on today. The Parade holds pride of place in this photograph, but it is still worth having a glance at the beautiful scroll work and arcades of the Town Hall.

Above: We are a good ten years on from the end of the Cold War between the USA and the USSR, but from the late 1940s people lived with it as an everyday reality. Britain's own nuclear weapons, and the presence of American bases in our country, put Britain in the front line of any potential conflict. Most people accepted this as a fact of life, but the Campaign for Nuclear Disarmament (CND) vigorously opposed all nuclear weapons. 'Ban the Bomb' was the famous chant and equally famous was its logo. The first of the local CND protests took place at Wood Hill in 1962 and the tactics adopted were to become the hallmark of the movement - the 'sit down' protest. The policeman on the right is trying to talk the girl into moving, but no doubt she too will soon have to be dragged away to the Black Maria. Both girls have the typical scarves and duffel coats of student protesters of the day. Some of the customers of the Black Boy Hotel have bagged a grandstand view and the bus passengers are bemused by it all. It was easy to ridicule young idealists, but this was 1962, the year of the Cuban Missile Crisis - no laughing matter.

Below: Shoppers could have been excused for blinking twice at the surprising scene which greeted them in a town centre shop window sometime in 1967. After all, it is not too often that a bikini clad beauty takes a bath in public, and no doubt one or two husbands were frog-marched away by angry wives for their apparent sudden interest in beauty products. This is what local girl and professional model, Jackie Mills, was promoting. She did not stay there too long - she might have started a riot - but she certainly got the 'fame for 15 minutes' which Andy Warhol predicted everyone would have in the modern age of mass communications. Of course this was the 'swinging sixties', which was arguably the most socially transforming decade of the century. The mini-skirt, the 'pill', the Beatles, LSD - it all seemed light years away from the restrictive 1950s. Not only this, some of the most memorable political events belonged to this decade. If you lived through it, can you forget the terrible fear engendered by the Cuban Crisis? Can you ever forget that day in Dallas when President Kennedy died? But for all that, it wasn't every day that you found a girl bathing in a shop window!

***Left:** Is it never going to start? This seems to be the thought written across the face of the young girl in the middle of the front row as this crowd of youngsters awaits the Punch and Judy show. The scene is the Abington Park Show in the early 1950s, and the limits of the fun you can get from swinging on a rope barrier look as if they have just about been reached. Never mind - no doubt the doleful expressions turned to delight as soon as Mr Punch squawked into action. The spacious Abington Park, with its boating lakes and pleasant walks, was once the private estate of Lady Wantage. In 1897, on the occasion of Queen Victoria's Diamond Jubilee, she presented the park to the town and retired to Overstone. Since then, it has provided the opportunity for fresh air and relaxation 'on the doorstep' for thousands of Northamptonians. During the Second World War, Abington Park became the venue for some of the 'Holidays at Home' entertainments. These were laid on by the local council during the summer holiday weeks because wartime travel restrictions and petrol shortages made getting away so difficult. After the war these annual events gradually evolved into the 'Town Show.'*

***Above:** It's a happy looking rehearsal, although everybody seems to be doing pretty much their own thing'. The most instantly recognisable figure is Des O'Connor, and not far behind in this respect is Jim Dale, next but one to Des. Both these showbiz celebrities have local connections. Des was an evacuee who spent most of his early years in Northampton, whilst Jim hails from nearby Rothwell. Des was a redcoat at a holiday camp at which he won a national talent contest. To celebrate, he appeared at a show at the ABC Cinema, along with Jim Dale and others. The photograph has captured a cheerful moment during rehearsals for the show, which hairstyles and fashions would suggest was in the late 60s. The girl on the right is singing along with Des, whilst the others are simply enjoying the joke, although the girl to the left of Des seems to be suffering from 'rehearsal fright'. Des went on to have a hugely successful career as a comedian and singer; more lately as a chat show host. His appearance has remained remarkably unaltered over the years. Jim Dale first made his mark as a 'pop' singer, but he is perhaps better known now for his comedy appearances in 'Carry On ...' films.*

On the move

Below: A long line of coaches belonging to local firm Wesley's stretches its way along the side of Market Square almost to Burtons in the background. This scene was captured on a hot summer's day in the 1960s, and obviously an outing of some considerable size was being undertaken in what would have been luxury coaches of their day. The first coach is parked outside the very pleasant frontage of Faulkner and Alsop (Solicitors) and this was once Beethoven House, a music school. The following three coaches stand before Victor Value Supermarket and a very mundane block of offices. Only a few years earlier, however, this site had been occupied by the very fine Peacock Hotel, an old coaching inn, which was demolished in 1961. Strangely enough, the supermarket and office block in the photograph was itself bulldozed at a later date to make way for Peacock Place. Perhaps it should have been called Peacock's Revenge! The Market Square presents a motley collection of period vehicles in the photograph, including an A35 van, an A40 Farina and a Ford Anglia.

Right: Traffic jams come in all shapes and sizes, but a cyclist always has a chance of sneaking through somehow. For many years the level crossing at Cotton End provided an unwelcome obstacle for those travelling between the town centre and Far Cotton. Those precious few minutes could be vital, especially for those needing to clock in at work on time. This 1950s shot at Bridge Street shows an option that was not open to the motorists. Of course it could be a toss up as to whether it was actually worthwhile to hoist your bike on your shoulder and use the footbridge, or whether the gates might open just as you reached the top of the steps, but the grin on the face of one of the cyclists seems to indicate that he knows something that the others don't! There are a good few fashion pointers to suggest that this might be the early 1950s, not least the cycle clips to hold in the baggy trousers of that time. It was either that or tucking your trousers into your socks to avoid that oily chain. Cycling gear is much more streamlined today, but the problems of weaving a way through dense urban traffic have much increased.

GGK
437

Bottom: Many readers may have fond recollections of taking and passing their Cycling Proficiency Test at school. Perhaps their certificates are stuck in scrap-books, or in frames on walls, or maybe they have gone the way of many certificates and awards - into some black hole somewhere. Considerably fewer Northamptonians will have participated in the training scheme for motorcyclists which was instituted in the early 1960s by the RAC and local clubs. The photograph shows one of the instruction sessions in progress, with the policeman on the right keeping a close watch on the trainees pedestrian crossing behaviour. The bikes themselves are of considerable interest and all of them now could be classed as period pieces. The police patrolman is astride a quite powerful looking BSA whilst, in contrast, the lady learner is aboard an LE Velocette, known as a noddybike. The gentleman to the right of the trio of trainees has an interesting looking bulbous horn on his handlebars. The motorcycle apparel might have come straight from the window of Burtons or from the pages of Country Life magazine. Incredibly, although this scene pre-dated the compulsory wearing of crash helmets, nobody is wearing one, not even the policeman!

Right: Interested onlookers wonder what is going on, as workmen paint white rectangles on the kerbs in Sheep Street, but in the war anything could happen! As soon as World War Two began, a general blackout was enforced so as to give enemy bombers no obvious targets. Householders could buy Lightproof Bolton Sheeting at 3s 11d (19p) per yard. More likely, they would buy rolls of blackout paper from Boots Chemists at 1s 6d (7p), or even fashion their own. The need for a total blackout was felt to be vital and it was common to hear the cry of, 'Put that light out!' from Air Raid Wardens patrolling the streets. Prosecutions for failing to observe the blackout were common. The problem was that at first a spate of accidents occurred in the densely black streets. Therefore local councils had to have such things as lamp-posts and kerbs painted, at least partially, in white. Car owners had to line their bumpers and mudguards in white. The blackout had its uses, of course. It provided ideal cover for a spot of 'black marketeering' or, from 1942, for a lady to meet an American G I. 'Over paid, over sexed and over here,' they seemed to have endless supplies of such things as cigarettes and nylon stockings.

Shopping spree

Above: The long sweep of Sheep Street provides nothing more than an exercise in nostalgia now, for this row of small shops was demolished to provide a through road in conjunction with the Grosvenor Shopping Centre during 1971-72. This photograph was taken in 1963, and perhaps distance lends enchantment, but there seems to be something very attractive now about such a vista. Perhaps it is because the rise of superstores has made them an increasingly rare sight in the centres of our towns and cities. It is more than this. The appeal lies in the variety of building styles and the different roof levels, partly the result of houses being turned into shops or extensions 'tacked on' at various times. Superstores have their advantages, but in comparison their appearance seems bland and uniform. Quite a few readers may remember these names that were once to be found on Sheep Street - Valentine Charles Ltd (wines and spirits); Frosts (children's shop); Sigwart's (with the pointing finger to help you). Last but not least, below the Mackeson sign, was the ideal place to rest weary feet and take a little refreshment - Ron's Wine, Beer and Coffee Tavern.

Top: Don't they know there's a war on? In spite of shortages and rationing, this busy Market Square scene from the early 1940s shows that people were determined to get out and see what they could snap up. And why not the luxury of some ice-cream? It would have to be Gallones of course, a household name in Northampton. Wartime shopping, as readers who experienced it will remember, required an endless supply of optimism. Coupons were needed for shoes and clothing, along with a range of foodstuffs that had been plentiful before the war. Many items simply disappeared from the shelves, never to be seen until after the war. The humble banana, for example, was a thing of fancy and imagination. The great hope was, of course, that your friendly local shopkeeper might have a little bit of something extra - 'under the counter'. The hidden benefit (not appreciated by 1940s housewives) was that shortages of sugar and fat, along with plenty of home-grown vegetables, meant that the diet of that day was probably healthier than that of today. There are some very distinctive marks of the 1940s on the photograph, not least the boneshaker prams and the sturdy Wolseley car with wartime headlight mask.

& LESLIE
ESTER ASSURANCE
BURTON

Left: It's a lively scene of human activity in the Market Square in the 1950s. The stalls are thronged and a hand-cart awaits to help unload the contents of the wagon marked 'Tomkins Seeds.' The handsome building outside which the wagon is parked is 'The Peacock.' This was an old coaching inn with stabling for 30 horses, a feature of the Square. As part of Northampton's heritage, it provided a link to the time when the horse was the speediest form of transport and the Market Square would echo to the sound of hooves and coach wheels on the cobbles. Unfortunately 'The Peacock' stood in the way of 1960s 'progress', a time when scant regard was given to continuity and tradition in the quest for modernity. This historic building was bulldozed in order to make way for a featureless office block in 1961. A 1990s shot from the same angle would reveal much that is different. That is to be expected of the centre of any twentieth century town or city. However one feature provides a constant on the skyline, the impressive Town Hall tower. The statue on the right-hand gable of the building is that of St Michael, patron saint of corporations.

Below: Could this be the New Year sales at George Mence Smith Ltd, Ironmongers? Is there a rush on to grab a bargain gardening spade or some other such exotic item? The truth of the matter was that news had got around about certain items of clothing being off-ration and available for purchase without clothing coupons. Hence this gigantic queue at Lyons clothing shop on Mercers Row. This was, of course, the 1940s and the styles of dress on the photograph bear this out, as does the splendid tandem pram. It is difficult to envisage a time when you had only 66 coupons for clothes for a whole year, unless you lived through it. For a man, a shirt would set you back five coupons, trousers eight coupons and a jacket 13 coupons. Rationing on food was introduced early in 1940 and on clothing in June 1941. To save on materials and manpower, Utility Clothing had to be made, lacking embroidery and trimmings, and with limited pleats, seams and buttonholes. The garments were stamped with the symbol CC41 (Civilian Clothing 1941). It all sounds very grim and austere, but there were ways and means around the system - spivs and the black market for example.

Bottom: A wonderful atmosphere of bustle and activity is evoked in this shot of Market Square showing an open-air market as it really should be. Masses of people are seeking that little bit of extra value for money, or even a real bargain, and you can almost hear the stall-holders shouting out their special offers or exchanging banter with prospective customers. For many people in this photograph, the outing to market will have been not merely a shopping trip, but a social occasion, a chance to meet friends and have a gossip. Modern shopping centres have their advantages, but they seem anonymous and lifeless in comparison to the good old-fashioned open-air market. The busy scene pre-dates 1962, for that was the year in which the centre point of Market Square, the fountain, was dismantled. Some familiar names of the time may be seen on the premises in the background. On the left is Roses Fashion Centre in Waterloo House; then Phoenix Assurance; then Phelan and Agutter, Estate Agents. On the right-hand side of the Square the names of Pearl Assurance and Liptons are visible. The distinctive tower and cupola of All Saints Church dominates the skyline, with the dome of the Westminster Bank to the right.

Right: The 1960s Market Square shoppers perhaps took the backdrop of buildings for granted, unaware that soon all was to change. In 1972 this whole side of the Square was demolished to make way for the Grosvenor Centre, including the two buildings featured. To the left, the Emporium Arcade was a fine piece of Edwardian architecture, built in 1908, with an attractive two-toned frontage of bricks. The 1930s building to the right was home to Northampton's daily 'Chronicle and Echo' and the weekly 'Mercury and Herald.' This had been the site of Northampton newspapers since the 1740s, and the 'Mercury' boasts the record of being the oldest continuous newspaper in the United Kingdom, never having missed an edition since its founding in 1720. The council's proposals to build a new shopping centre, and in so doing destroy fine buildings and historic links, met with fierce opposition. The 'Chronicle and Echo' itself spearheaded the campaign, and a Civic Society was set up to try and preserve the area. Nevertheless the proposals went through, and only the figure of the horseman on the current newspaper offices in Upper Mounts Street reminds us of the time when couriers clattered into Market Square with the first news from the south.

The clock on the Emporium Arcade stands at midday on a sunny Saturday in July 1966. Market Square presents a busy scene as the various stalls attract plenty of custom. The buildings to the rear give an impression of solidity and permanence, but within six years they were gone and this aspect of the Square had changed dramatically. With the buildings having been constructed at different times, each had its own stamp of individuality. Abel's Records, with the Pye logo beneath the name, was housed in a simple building that had been in business as a music shop since 1790. The Emporium Arcade, with its wonderful frontage of two-tone brickwork, had been erected in 1908. A relative newcomer to the scene was the structure which accommodated the offices of the 'Chronicle and Echo' and the 'Mercury and Herald'. This had been built in the 1930s. The overall effect was one of variety and great interest, as is often the case when buildings have different origins over a long span of time. In 1972 the row was demolished to make way for the Grosvenor Shopping Centre, completely changing the character of this end of Market Square.

At work

Perched aloft on their scaffolding, these workmen are getting a close-up view which very few will have been able to enjoy. They may not be particularly appreciating the privilege, for it must have been hard work giving these Town Hall statues a wash and brush up, as captured in this photograph which dates back to the 1950s. Northampton Town Hall, the administrative heart of the town, was opened in 1863. It had been designed by Godwin, with extensions coming at later stages, the second section being designed by Matthew Holding. The building is noted for the wonderful carvings and statuary on its facade. These 14 life size statues, each with an elaborate canopy, represent famous figures from Northampton's history. They are truly beautiful examples of craftsmanship and it seems a pity that, for the most part, only the birds can regularly appreciate them at close quarters. The Town Hall is in good company, for just as impressive in its own way is the stately tower and cupola of All Saints Church in the background. Northampton can be proud of its 14 famous citizens, but it can also take great pride in the fine architecture which graces this part of the town.

NORTHAMPTON TOWN HALL, THE ADMINISTRATIVE HEART OF THE TOWN WAS OPENED IN 1863

Below: The police sergeant looks as if he is giving the little boy a severe interrogation, but the kindly smile on the face of his colleague gives the game away. It is a case of a little boy lost and the constabulary coming to the rescue. This touching little scene was captured by Roland Holloway in George Row, near All Saints Church, in the 1930s.
The day appears to be a chilly one, judging by the clothes on view, and the policemen in particular are well clad against the weather. They would have to be, for this was a time when most constables would be found pounding the pavement rather than in patrol cars - cold work in winter. A 'bobby on the beat', of course, had a good chance of picking up on a tearful toddler in distress whose expression gives every indication that he thinks the end of the world has come. Rescue was probably imminent, for apparently All Saints Church was a good place for mothers to be re-united with lost infants. On a little period note - it is always surprising to see a belisha beacon and pedestrian crossing studs in the relatively traffic-free 1930s.

Left: One year short of its centenary and the famous Market Square fountain has been felled. The scene is April 1962 and the cast-iron column, along with its four drinking bowls, its cattle troughs and its bronze decorations lies ready to be disposed of. The argument to justify this action was that the fountain had become fragile and dangerous. Nevertheless, it took a team of men, along with modern equipment, two days to get it down. The workmanship on this fragile Victorian treasure can clearly be seen on the photograph, and the men on the plinth are struggling with what appear to be the drinking bowls. The youngsters are enjoying all the excitement, but the action of the council caused an outcry locally. It seemed to many that this was wanton destruction of part of Northampton's heritage. Unhappily the 1960s was a time when town planners, eager to look forward, tended to believe that progress necessarily depended upon sweeping away the past wholesale. Conservation was a concept that was scarcely recognised. A competition was held for the purpose of replacing the fountain. The winning entry was for a proposed structure to be named 'The Fountain of Light', by Willi Soukop, but it came to nothing.

Above: This was a memorable day for the Manfield Orthopaedic Hospital in 1930, and particularly for the boy scout troop which had been formed there that year. The notable visitors, who had come with the express purpose of giving a boost to the scouts, were members of the Australian cricketing tour party. The famous Don Bradman was amongst them. The Australian guests can be seen in the lighter suits, all looking very smart, and Bradman is in the foreground to the left. One of scouting's highest awards is to individual scouts who struggle successfully against adversity. In the case of these hospitalised scouts they surely all deserved the award. The two on crutches are proudly wearing their troop neckerchiefs and each has the scout badge in his lapel. Cricketing fans or not, they were probably thrilled to be meeting the 'Don' who, at 22, had become a legend already.
In this 1930 tour of England, his test match average was an incredible 139.14 runs. His score of 334 in one test innings was not bettered until Len Hutton's 364 in 1938. Don Bradman was probably the greatest batsman of all time and perhaps his visit encouraged these scouts to even more determination.

Right: It must have been a fine view of the centre of Northampton from up there, but a modern safety inspector would have a fit. The two workmen appear to be enjoying their ride on the huge bucket of bricks, but there is not a safety helmet in sight. Also, at some stage, the one with the cigarette in his mouth is going to have to cling on one-handed if he is actually going to smoke it! The date was 1946, and although there was little to be done in the way of repairing bomb damage, there was still improvement work on the menu. This particular scheme was concerned with demolishing the buildings that formed a bottleneck in Abington Street. The workers could enjoy the sight of some distinguished looking buildings from an unusual perspective. To the right, the fine looking building with the roof gables belonged to Doffmans. The succession of signs advertised the variety of their clothing operations - 'Showrooms'; 'Cutter and Fitter'; 'Resistorm Weathercoats'; 'Granby Raincoats'; 'Ladies' Tailors'. This 1946 project was perhaps a straw in the wind' for the substantial redevelopment of the town centre in the 60s and 70s.

WATERLOO HOUSE
CENTRE
DOFFMAN'S
ENTRANCE
3
ABINGTON ST
DOFFMAN'S
LADIES TAILORS
DOFFMAN'S
GRANBY
RAINCOATS
DOFFMAN
RESISTORM
WEATHERCOATS
DOFFMAN
CUTTER & FITTER
DOFFMAN'S
SHOWROOMS

British Timken - bearing itself proudly after a hundred years' success

A century ago, many thousands of miles away from Northampton, a carriage builder named Henry Timken, with his sons William and Henry (known as H H) and nephew Reginald Heinzleman, set up a new, separate company in the blacksmith shop of his main business,The Timken Carriage Company in St Louis. The new company was named The Timken Roller Bearing Axle Company, so is not difficult to hazard a guess as to what it produced. In fact, the axles were equipped with tapered roller bearings of Henry Timken's own invention, designed to reduce axle friction in horse-drawn carriages. Henry Timken had, during his career, registered 13 patents for successful innovations in the carriage-building industry, but the tapered roller bearings which he developed when he was in his 60s were the most significant invention of all.

Above: *Henry Timken.*
Below: *A 1940s view of the staff and directors with Sir John Pascoe centre left.*

Soon the company was also making tapered roller bearings for the embryonic motor car industry, working with automotive pioneers including Olds and Packard; and when Henry Ford introduced the affordable Model T in 1908 and improved the assembly-line method of manufacture, car production began to increase and axle production at Timken increased with it.

Timken's first overseas production was authorised in 1909 when a licence was granted to the Electric & Ordnance Accessories Company Limited, a subsidiary of Vickers Ltd, to produce Timken bearings and market axle sets in England. Production began at Cheston Road, Aston, where at first tapered roller bearings represented just a small sideline among the factory's other products. However, imported horse drawn vehicle axle sets found a ready market among the makers of wagons and carriages, and before long the company was supplying bearings to the early British motor car manufacturers - Daimler, Darracq, Sentinel Steam Waggon, Mann's Steam Car, Jefferies Electric Vehicle and others.

Sales volume increased steadily, as did the number of different sizes of bearings manufactured; in 1910 there were 12 sizes, with the largest not exceeding 5" outside diameter, and by 1911 the range had increased to around 60 different sizes. Development continued during World War I; automobile bearings,

originally used for hubs, had now found a variety of applications, and bearings were also required for use in tanks. In 1917, shortage of space prompted Vickers to reorganise Electric and Ordnance Accessories Limited, and the Timken section was moved to Wolseley Motors Limited at Common Lane, Birmingham. Here, by the end of the war, bearings up to eight and a half inches in diameter were being manufactured; production was still under 4,000 bearings a week and the workforce numbered less than 100, but demand for tapered roller bearings was increasing rapidly. On June 4 1920, British Timken Limited, a subsidiary of Messrs Wolseley Motors Limited, was formed.

Above, both pictures: *The Timken Show was for many years an important part of the company's calendar. Here we see two sides of the events from the 1940s.*

A major reorganisation of the Vickers group in 1927 led to the signing of an agreement with the American parent company The Timken Roller Bearing Company. Under this agreement British Timken Limited became a joint enterprise between Vickers and The Timken Roller Bearing Company, under the Chairmanship of Mr Michael Dewar. The new company moved back into its original premises in Cheston Road, Aston, where production rose to some 5,000 bearings a week. It was many years later, in 1959, that the Timken Roller Bearing Company acquired full ownership of British Timken.

The range of bearings continued to expand and diversify, with tapered roller bearings for steam railway locomotives introduced into production in 1928, followed by heavy rolling mill bearings and bearings for the aircraft industry in 1931. Continuous development and improvement of equipment and manufacturing methods ensured that the company maintained the reputation which it had by now built up as the manufacturer of the finest anti-friction bearings in Europe. With an increasing number of manufacturers using British-made bearings, the workforce was growing to keep up with demand; by 1937 over 1,000 people were employed. The company had also set up its first manufacturing subsidiary overseas; British Timken SA (pty) Limited was formed in Johannesburg in South Africa in 1932. Initially concentrating on the production of a large variety of components for the specialised tapered roller bearings applications in mines, this factory was soon supplying the many other industries of the African continent.

The outbreak of war in 1939 brought a sharp acceleration in the demand for bearings of all kinds, and Timken expanded into the manufacture of ball bearings with the acquisition of the Fischer Bearings Company Limited at Wolverhampton (subsequently disposed of to the Fafnir Bearing Co (GB) Ltd). Shadow factories were set up for both these factories so that if the main sites were to be hit during the increasingly heavy air raids on Birmingham, production would not be brought to a halt. A disused factory at Coalville, Leicestershire, was equipped to manufacture a cross-section of Timken's output, and Fischer Bearings' dispersal scheme operated in an old tile works at Hednesford and an old enamelling works at Bilston. The enamelling works was equipped as a shadow heat treatment shop, and within 24 hours of the arrangements being made the existing heat treatment shop was hit by a German bomb.

At the end of the war, the Coalville and Bilston factories were closed down and staff and equipment transferred back to the other factories. Additional capacity was now provided by a new plant at Duston. Building work had commenced at this site in 1941, against the background of the second world war, and the Duston plant had begun production five and a half months later, in 1942. Development and expansion was to continue at Duston for the next 15 years, however; the factory was extended to more than twice its original size, and it was not until 1957 - the year of the inauguration of British Railway's high-speed London to Edinburgh service, operating the first passenger rolling stock in the country to be converted from plain bearing axleboxes to British Timken's tapered roller bearing axleboxes - that the office block was finished and the building was declared complete.

The progress of the building extensions at Duston had been recorded year by year in The Timken Times, the company's monthly magazine which was produced from 1946 on, giving news of the company's achievements both at home and overseas, reports of sporting and other events, and articles on various aspects of the company. An update of the building work, with a photograph, was included in the Christmas edition each year, culminating in a proud announcement in the

Above, both pictures: *Two delightful views of the Timken Show.*

March 1957 edition, 'Building Complete at Duston'. Photographs showed the Technical Department on the first floor and the Sales Department on the ground floor, as well as the impressive factory frontage, and the offices were described as 'light and airy' and the conditions as 'ideal'. Indeed, employees have always found British Timken a good place to work. The Timken Times regularly paid tribute to long-serving employees at Duston and elsewhere; in 1967 121 employees qualified for their gold watch to mark 21 years' service, and in 1977, 115 gold watches were presented; this brought the total number of employees who had received watches since awards began in 1948 to 1,434, of whom 835 were still with the company.

The fact that so many employees choose to stay with the company is due in no small part to British Timken's long-standing commitment to training, which Sir John Pascoe, the Company's distinguished Managing Director until 1960, saw as being vital to the strength of British industry. As early as 1957, the company distributed a brochure outlining its four systems of apprenticeship - craft, student, technical and graduate - which attracted enquiries from as far afield as Edinburgh, Cardiff and Belfast. The apprenticeship scheme included such modern concepts as day-release, graduate entry and even equal opportunities, with provision made for female as well as male trainees.

Enjoying excellent career prospects from the early days, the workforce at Duston also benefited from the very active British Timken Social and Athletic Club, which provided first-class facilities to its members and made a valued contribution to all local sporting activities. The range of activities on offer catered for most tastes, with less strenuous sports such as bowls and fishing, and more unusual ones such as archery. The athletics section even had its own running track, opened by HRH The Duke of Edinburgh on December 15 1954, being acclaimed at the time as one of the best in the country. British Timken today still has fine sports facilities, with bowling rinks, tennis courts, floodlit football pitch and a cricket ground. Its cricket team enjoyed a particularly strong reputation. In 1951 British Timken sponsored a new cricket league, the Northamptonshire County Cricket League, with the object of raising the standard of club cricket in Northamptonshire; it then proceeded to top the League with great regularity.

To many people, Timken is perhaps best remembered for the Timken Show. The first Timken Show was staged in 1945, and then went on to become one of the leading shows in Britain before being phased out in the 1970s. Attractions at the early Shows included a Horse and Pony Gymkhana, a Horticultural Show with £85 in prize money, a Handicraft Show, a Baby Show and of course the Timken Exhibition marquees with display stands by the leading engineering firms in Northampton. Held primarily for the

Left: *A member of the Inspection department at Duston prior to automation in 1950.* ***Above left:*** *The technical department.*

enjoyment of its workers and for the benefit of selected charities, the Timken Show set out 'to give all comers a very excellent day's entertainment', which it accomplished so successfully that it attracted more and more visitors each year, quickly fulfiling the early organisers' wish that one day 'the fame of our Show Day will emulate that of the Chelsea Flower Show and the British Industries Fair rolled into one'. By 1957 the two-day show was attracting 30,000 visitors, and one of the show-jumping competitions was being televised by the BBC. Held on the company's sports ground which had by now grown to 70 acres, the Show's events that year included judo and gymnastic displays, an exhibition of agricultural machinery, sheep dog demonstrations, a dog show, a livestock show with classes for cattle, sheep and pigs, a horticultural show, Best Child's Pony classes, Light Utility Turnouts and Hackneys, Trotting Races, and show jumping events for juniors and seniors. The Show was attended by many well-known personalities, particularly from the show-jumping world; famous faces to be seen there in 1957 included the Marquis and Marchioness of Northampton, Lt-Col Harry Llewelyn, Pat Smythe, Dorian Williams - and of course Tiger Timken, the company's mascot for many years, now retired. The 42,500 people who attended the 1970 show also saw the Red Devils air display, the Band of HM Royal Marines, Portsmouth, and top show-jumpers including Harvey Smith, David Broome riding Sportsman and Mrs Alison Dawes riding The Maverick.

One famous British horsewoman who has visited British Timken in an official rather than a sporting capacity is HRH Princess Anne. On her visit to Duston in 1972, the Princess opened an Industrial Rehabilitation Workshop built by the Northampton and County Junior Chamber of Commerce at St Crispins Hospital, Duston, before going on to British Timken, where she was received by the Lord Lieutenant of Northampton, Lt Col John Chandos-Pole, who presented S F Bennett, Chairman of British Timken, Mrs Bennett, and the Mayor and Mayoress of Northampton. The Princess' tour of the works included the Continuous Line Works which was the first automated bearing factory of its kind in Europe designed for the automatic manufacture of tapered roller bearings, factory units housing roller grinding, roller view, heat treatment, grinding and assembly operations, and the Apprentice Workshop. The Princess then left by helicopter from the British Timken Sportfield; observers noted that it was a Wessex helicopter and therefore, appropriately enough, equipped with British Timken bearings.

Top left: *Storing bearings during production.*
Top right: *Setter Machinist apprentice training.*
Left: *Tiger Timken, the now obsolete mascot.*

In 1965 the Nene Foundation was established as a charitable organisation which distributes grants for various charitable purposes in the communities in which employees of British Timken live. It receives funds for this purpose from the Timken International Fund which was set up by the three grandsons of the founder, Henry Timken. The income from the fund is distributed to various communities around the world. Since its inception in 1965 £4.4million has been donated to community projects in the Northampton and Daventry areas.

A British Timken employee named Mary Finch, who was Show Day Secretary for the third Timken Show, wrote in August 1947, "It would be an interesting, if an idle, speculation to conjure what the Company will be like at the dawn of the twenty-first century. I cannot imagine that the men and women who run it will be very different from ourselves. Almost certainly they will be better fed and better clothed; let us hope that they will be less harassed by fears, anxieties and shortages. Undoubtedly great strides will be made from the engineering point of view, and let us hope that those who have not already seen the light will have done so by then, and a general use of Timken tapered roller bearings will apply throughout the industry." As the twenty-first century approaches, we can judge for ourselves the accuracy of her speculation. Great strides have been made in engineering and British Timken's Duston factory is certainly different today as a result of continuing investment. Timken bearings are indeed now in general use across the world in all sectors of industry including aerospace on projects such as Concorde and the Space Shuttle. One thing however is unchanged and that is the commitment of the company and its workforce to its customers and to the community in which they reside.

Top: *The completed factory at Duston in 1957.*
Above left: *Princess Anne's visit to Duston in 1972.*
Below: *The visit of the Board of Directors to Duston in 1996. WR Timken (centre) is the fourth generation of the family to lead the business.*

Quinton House School - a story of success

The Red Lady and the Blue Lady, both in love with the same man; the lost village; the unearthly White Lady who circles the lake; the mysterious tale of the white peacock - stories of ghosts, mysteries and legends from the ancient past are part of the folklore of Quinton House School, formerly Upton Hall School. And what could be more understandable for an establishment whose own records are linked with a building whose history can be traced back to medieval times?

Ghosts and spirits, however, play little part in the day-to-day life of Quinton House in the 1990s, and if things go bump in the night the reason is likely to have more to do with the high spirits of children rather than the spirits of the long departed!

The school's own history goes back to 1946, when the three Misses Teape leased the rather run-down Upton Hall and opened a school on the premises, where well brought-up children - many of them the children of servicemen - could learn to sing, dance, play the piano and gain a basic education. Before the school opened, Upton Hall, which then belonged to Sir Thomas White's Charity Trust, had fallen into a state of disrepair and was almost hidden from view among the badly overgrown grounds and driveway. The nearby woodland had expanded and spread into the grounds, and self-set elder and sycamore trees had crept relentlessly towards the hall. Few people at that time were interested in renovating such large properties and their adjoining acres of land; the second world war had recently ended and post-war prosperity in Britain was still a long way off.

By the summer of 1947 Upton Hall School was ready to take its very first pupils, two young girls. With honour, discipline and diligence as its principles, the school officially opened in the

Above: *The memorial to Jane Harrington nee Samwell in MIlton Church.*
Below: *South view of Upton Hall as it was in the last century.*

autumn, with seven boarders and around the same number of day girls. Boarders were taken from the age of five. Both girls and boys were accepted by the school, with a five percent reduction for sisters and brothers attending at the same time, though boys were only admitted up to the age of ten.

The physical and spiritual health of pupils featured high on Miss Teape's list of priorities. Games, including tennis, cricket, hockey, netball, rounders and swimming, were played every day, and the school doctor attended regularly. The prospectus described the diet as 'liberal, varied and very nourishing' and the children's meals benefited from the vegetables, fresh fruit and salads that were grown in the school's own four acres of kitchen garden and orchard.
The children attended St Michael's, the charming little Norman church nearby, every Sunday and were prepared for confirmation if the parents wished it.

Above: *The Hudson family were the last private owners of Upton Hall from 1893 - 1946.* ***Right:*** *The Church of St. Michael was endowed by families at the hall. It is now looked after and used by Quinton House School.*

Miss Teape retired in 1962, and Upton Hall School was taken over by Mr and Mrs MacDonald. The sixties saw a nationwide rebellion among young people, who began to demand freedom from authority and control. A strict discipline was retained, however, at Upton Hall.

Senior girls were allowed to go shopping in Northampton on Saturdays only, and then only with the consent of their parents. And woe betide any of the girls who were seen speaking to a boy!

The happiness of the pupils, however, was of great importance, and 'old girls' who revisited the school recently assured the present staff that they had thoroughly enjoyed their school life.

Quinton House came into being after the death of Mrs MacDonald, when Miss Madden took over as head teacher in September 1963 and renamed the school. Boarders were taken from the age of six to sixteen and Miss Madden set out to create a homely atmosphere for the children.

Above: *Stucco work in the ballroom done by Buggatti & Artari in 1737 portrays the Greek god Mercury - the messenger.* ***Top:*** *A scenic view of the school.* ***Left:*** *The 14th century timbered roof where some of the history of the school is taught.*

Another policy was that of personal tidiness, grooming and good manners. At the end of every day each child had to have a wash and brush up and be checked for tidiness by the teacher before leaving for home. Most classes had their own bathroom, and each child's hair brush, comb and towel were laid out there on individual trays.

Though the children were expected to be well mannered, this did not check their high spirits - or stop the odd childish prank such as piling books on top of a door ready to fall on the head of the first member of staff to walk through it!

A range of sporting activities was offered to the pupils of Quinton House, though the equipment and facilities were in fact rather limited. Running took place along the main driveway, netball was played on a small gravelled play area (disastrous to the knees of any child who happened to fall!) and tennis was relegated to an area near the lake. An interesting comment from a former member of staff was that the students of ballet, of which the school had many at the time, were not required to play hockey in case the dancers' legs were injured.

In 1976 Mr and Mrs Hoskison took over from Miss Madden and decided to admit senior boys for the first time. A new air of adventure, danger and enthusiasm suddenly hit the school, and the staff and pupils alike had to accustom themselves to their presence which brought a refreshingly different atmosphere to the school. Sporting facilities were enhanced by the addition of new hard surface tennis courts.

The Borough Council took over the administration of Upton Hall in 1986, when the Northampton Development Corporation was wound up. It was decided that the buildings should be re-roofed, and the old tiles were accordingly removed. Disaster struck during the night, when an unexpected storm brought a deluge that soaked desks, carpets, cloakrooms, blackboards and books.

Exams were imminent and work had to go on; sodden carpets were rolled up and carried away, text books were dried out, and the children did their best to concentrate on lessons while workmen clambered about overhead, disturbing the wet plaster that fell from the ceilings on to their work. Staff soldiered on with damp blackboards and soggy pieces of chalk.

In 1988 Mr and Mrs Griffiths took charge of the school. It was growing swiftly at the time, and in response to the expansion a number of rearrangements were made at Quinton House; senior students were placed in the Hall itself, while the junior school was moved to the Lindens, an old stable block which had been brought into use. The changes allowed a new nursery unit to be developed, and quarters suitable for such young children were constructed.

The following year saw the formation of the Parents Association, and a very first Christmas Ball was organised by two of the parents. Since then the Association has gone from strength to strength, organising fetes, 5th November bonfire celebrations, fathers v school cricket matches and open days.

Though fund raising is not their primary concern, the Association has provided much-needed drama equipment and stacking chairs for the assembly hall.

Sport has always taken an important place in the school curriculum, and in 1990 it was decided to lay a new football pitch in what had been the old walled garden. An overgrown area of thistles and weeds, the site seemed to be an ideal choice. What could be simpler? Clear it and level the ground.... Things turned out to be far more complicated than that, however. It appeared that the Saxons had at one time built a pottery there, and as the walled garden contained a site of historical importance it was not possible to level the ground completely. The sports pitch was built, though with a significant gradient that was to make itself felt among those teams who had to play uphill!

By 1992 Mr and Mrs Griffiths felt that if the school was to develop as they wanted, they needed to add a sixth form in order to offer their students more advanced studies. The new facility added a further dimension to the school - not all of it desirable, such as loud music echoing from the Sixth Form Common Room! In time, the first of the sixth formers graduated and went on to university life or to further professional training within their field of employment.

The basic principles on which Quinton House School was founded still hold good today. Hard work, discipline and good manners are as important today as ever, though more freedom of expression is encouraged. A family atmosphere is still fostered within the school, and the staff

firmly believe in valuing each pupil as an individual. Personal integrity and care and compassion for others are cultivated, and this is reflected in the school's commitment to a wide variety of charity works. Each House at the Hall chooses a charity to support each year, including such diverse works as riding for the disabled, sponsoring animals at Twycross Zoo, leukaemia in children, the Higgins Fund for AIDS, Northampton Soup Kitchen, Children in Need, Red Nose Day, research into breast cancer and many more. The junior school works just as hard for similar charities. They have raised money to provide alarms to prevent cot deaths, provided a guide dog for a blind person and helped children in need. The combined efforts throughout Quinton House School raises between £3,000 and £4,000 each year.

A wide curriculum is offered at Quinton House, and science, technology and information technology feature highly on the school's timetable. Computing facilities are available to all the pupils, and a specialist information technology unit offers the opportunity to keep abreast of today's developments. History and geography, music, science, elocution and dancing, art and craft all form part of the timetable. Religious Education is based on Christian teaching but tolerance and understanding of other faiths is promoted among the children from an early age. Languages include French, German and Spanish - in fact French is taught from the age of seven to give children a firm grasp of the subject.

Headmaster Gerald Griffiths and his staff can be justifiably proud of the students who leave Quinton House School as confident, well-balanced young men and women - and their commitment is to take the school forward into the next millennium with continued dedication to the highest possible standards.

Above: *Head Boy and Girl with younger pupils.*
Below: *The whole school in 1998.*
Facing page: *The girls' hockey team.*

The company with a lot of sole

At around the turn of the century Northampton, with its many leather tanneries and thriving boot and shoe industry, was known as the footwear capital of England. There were large manufacturers and there were small ones, and one of the very small manufacturers at this time must have been Mr Benjamin Griggs, who in 1901 started making boots, aided by Mr Septimus Jones, in a building at the side of his house, next to the gannick in High Street. He made the best of what facilities he had; the premises allowed him no space for an indoor packing area, so he would pack the finished boots, 12 dozen pairs to a box, in the yard outside, with no roof but the sky, boasting that he had the largest packing room in the world. He also enlisted the help of his family; his little daughter Nancy had the vital job of keeping her father supplied with tacks while he worked, which meant taking tacks out of the big pocket in her apron a handful at a time and holding them in her mouth until they were required. Benjamin's son Reginald also became involved in the business, and it was he who, after his father's death, finished building the factory which his father had started. The company has remained on this site in High Street and Cobb's Lane ever since.

From the beginning, Griggs' concentrated on making durable, hard-wearing boots and shoes from good quality materials and soon established a reputation as manufacturer of well-made, high quality footwear. The first boots made by the firm were leather soled and hob nailed, with riveted, screwed and stitched soles, with external and internal steel caps, and were directed at the industrial and safety footwear market. One of the firm's first lines to became a household name was the Bulldog boot, which was produced in the early 30s. These were boots of superior quality with seven inch legs, designed for agricultural and military use, and they became very popular amongst the gentlemen farmers in the North of England. They acquired the name Bulldog, so the story goes, when the sales agent in Leicester, who bred bulldogs, won Best In Show at Crufts; from then on, for as long as these boots were manufactured, every pair carried the Bulldog label.

However, the brand name amongst boots which everybody recognises today is Dr Martens. The circumstances which led to the invention of the famous air-cushion sole will be familiar to those reading this who have bought a pair of Docs and read the accompanying literature: in 1945 Dr Klaus Maerten, an orthopaedic surgeon in Germany, damaged his foot in a skiing accident. He was subsequently unable to find a pair of shoes which did not hurt his injured foot, so a college friend, Herbert Funck, brought his technical and engineering skills to bear on the problem, and between them they developed an air-cushion sole. Having solved Klaus Maerten's problem, they then put their invention into production in Seeshaupt, near Munich, with the assistance of a workforce which included an organ builder, a carpenter, a locksmith, a musician and a tailor. The basic materials used in the manufacture of the soles were redundant war materials: a substance called Igelit, which was used to repair the bodies of

Above: *Mr Benjamin R Griggs who founded the company in 1901.*

early aircraft, was welded around sponge rubber to produce a smooth and virtually indestructible sole. The design was patented and by the mid 50s Dr Maerten's boots were being sold in modest quantities across the Continent.

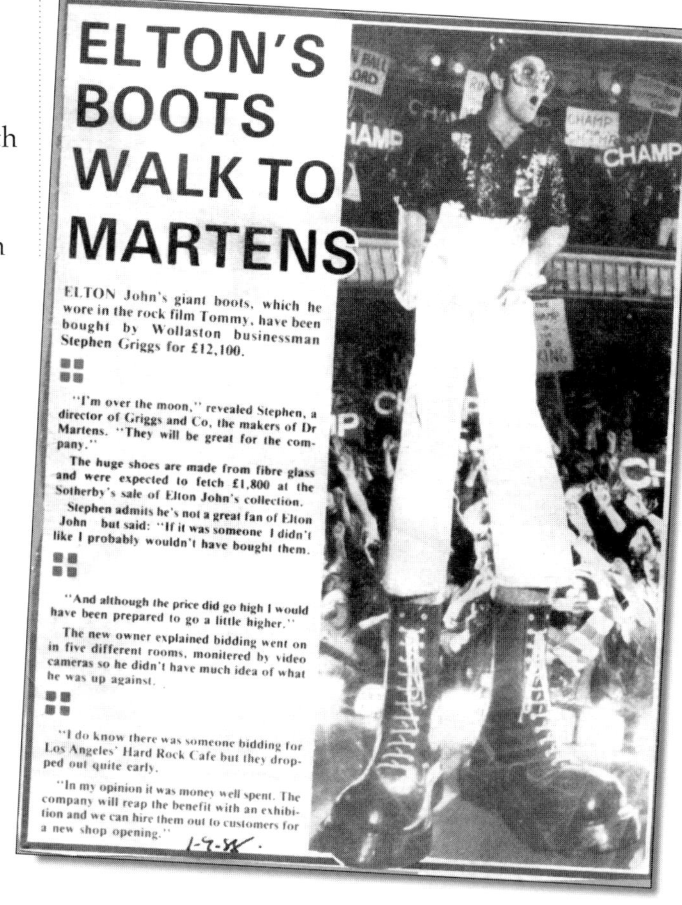

ELTON'S BOOTS WALK TO MARTENS

ELTON John's giant boots, which he wore in the rock film Tommy, have been bought by Wollaston businessman Stephen Griggs for £12,100.

"I'm over the moon," revealed Stephen, a director of Griggs and Co, the makers of Dr Martens. "They will be great for the company."

The huge shoes are made from fibre glass and were expected to fetch £1,800 at the Sotherby's sale of Elton John's collection.

Stephen admits he's not a great fan of Elton John but said: "If it was someone I didn't like I probably wouldn't have bought them.

"And although the price did go high I would have been prepared to go a little higher."

The new owner explained bidding went on in five different rooms, monitered by video cameras so he didn't have much idea of what he was up against.

"I do know there was someone bidding for Los Angeles' Hard Rock Cafe but they dropped out quite early.

"In my opinion it was money well spent. The company will reap the benefit with an exhibition and we can hire them out to customers for a new shop opening."

When the Dr Maerten franchise was offered to Great Britain's shoe manufacturers in the late 1950s, it met with widespread scepticism. Reginald Grigg's sons Bill and Ray were alone in recognising the tremendous commercial potential of Dr Maerten's invention. The brothers were very receptive to innovative ideas, and had in fact already become involved in the production of cost efficient vulcanised soles, having formed the Wollaston Vulcanising Cooperative during the 1950s. They eagerly entered into an agreement with Dr Klaus Maerten and Dr Ing. Herbert Funck which gave Griggs exclusive manufacturing rights of the air cushion sole, initially for a trial period of a year. In 1960 the factory in Cobb's Lane, Wollaston was ready to commence production of the boots, the name of which had, with the agreement of the inventors, been anglicised to Dr Martens, and the first pair of Dr Martens 1460s was produced on 1st April 1960. At first the boots were produced at a rate of around a thousand a month, by a workforce of less than 100. It took around 18 months to perfect the technique, as some initial problems were encountered in attaching the soles without a split appearing on the sole edge. However, at the end of the trial year the company had no hesitation in entering into a permanent franchise.

Functional, practical and distinctive, the boots were instantly adopted by the disaffected, anti-establishment British youth culture of the day and became an essential part of its dress code. As a result Dr Martens unexpectedly acquired a subversive, exciting image, associated with juvenile delinquence and anarchy. This high-profile street-cred image has stayed with Dr Martens through successive youth cultures, with Mods,

Top left: *Chairman Mr Bill Griggs.*
Top right: *Elton John wearing Dr Martens. One of many stars been seen in these famous shoes.*
Left: *The company premises.*

THE PRINCE'S YOUTH BUSINESS TRUST

Help for young people in starting or developing their own businesses

The Prince's Youth Business Trust is a charitable trust that provides finance, business advice and marketing opportunities for unemployed 18-29 year olds to set up their own businesses. It provides help to those unable to get all the support they need elsewhere.

The Trust has already helped around 20,000 people from a wide variety of backgrounds. Some have never been employed, others recently made redundant; some have degrees, others no paper qualifications at all. Help is available in the form of bursaries, low interest loans and test marketing grants, as well as continuing practical advice on business management.

Further information on the work of the Prince's Youth Business Trust and details of how to apply for sponsorship is available from the Trust at the address shown overleaf.

Help for The Prince's Youth Business Trust

For 33 years, Dr Martens footwear has been a fulcrum of Britain's youth cultures. At various times an essential dress item for 'skinheads' and 'punks,' in recent years, newer ranges of Doc Martens shoes have also been adopted by a more affluent young market looking for style and value.

Aware that their success has been largely due to the loyalty of young people from all backgrounds, Dr. Martens decided to mark their 30th anniversary in 1990 by donating a total of £250,000 to The Prince's Youth Business Trust.

For 1990, Dr Martens produced a special Limited Edition of 1,000,000 pairs of shoes and boots and, for every pair sold, contributed 25p to the Trust.

Dr. Martens were also proud to be the first commercial organization to employ the PYBT's 'crowned C' motif on their sponsorship promotional materials.

The year's production of limited edition Dr. Martens were sold out in just ten months and have now become something of a collector's item.

Encouraged by this success and impressed by what they had seen of The Prince's Youth Business Trust at work, Dr. Martens decided to maintain their sponsorship of the PYBT.

Many events with young people in mind are now held by The Prince's Youth Business Trust with sponsorship by Dr. Martens. These include: the widely acclaimed catwalk displays at the Clothes Show Live, often featuring the popular Doctor Stuart, and the PYBT Trade Fair at the International Autumn Fair, where 200 companies each year that have been helped by the Trust sell very successfully to trade buyers; and the nation-wide Battle of the Bands, designed to give aspiring and talented young musicians a foot on the ladder of recording success.

These worthwhile events continue 'Docs' support for young people—support in a financial, as well as purely physical, sense!

Skinheads, Punks, Indie Kids and followers of Grunge all inseparable from their Docs. But while the youth culture was using its cherry-red bovver boots to make a statement, thousands of workmen and women were quietly wearing Docs because of their durability, comfort and value for money. Sales rose quickly, and there was never any doubt that Bill and Ray's decision to acquire exclusive rights to manufacture in the United Kingdom had been a wise one; employees travelling between Hinwick Road and the vulcanising plant can give thanks to the brothers' farsightedness each time they drive along Williams Way and Raymond Close. By 1990 Griggs' workforce had increased to over 1,200, sales had reached £40 million and the brand was becoming increasingly known internationally. By 1997 sales had risen to nearly £250 million.

As turnover has increased, so the role of the sales and marketing division, AirWair Ltd, has become more and more important. For a long time little or no brand marketing had been done by the company, but by 1993 Airwair had begun to establish an international distributor network and recognised the need for a single market strategy. The company planned to extend the range in order to broaden the appeal of the brand and present it to the trade in specific, well-defined product categories. This radical new approach was put to the test at the major international trade shows, and proved successful. AirWair then concentrated on building closer partnerships with its key retailers around the world, including them in AirWair's sales conferences to keep them fully in the picture on brand planning and new product development. The new marketing strategies were consolidated by the establishment of strong communications with the consumer, with the first message, 'Made Like No Other Shoe On Earth', launched in 1997, to excellent effect. AirWair is also responsible for the development and marketing of a select range of clothing and accessories.

However, footwear remains at the core of the company's activities, with its other industrial brand names 'GettaGrip' and 'Impact' just as well-respected, if not as well-known, as Dr Martens. A policy of continuous investment ensures that the essentially traditional British craft of boot and shoe making is supported by the best technology and equipment available. Millions of pounds have been invested in equipment from injection moulding machinery to production line track systems. The company wants every single pair of Dr Martens which comes off the production line to be fault-free. Development is on-going, with areas such as dual density polyurethane and the wrap-around sole unit for children's stitchdown shoes currently under investigation; and there is a

Top: *Dr Martens have donated £250,000 to the Prince's Youth Business Trust.*
Right: *The ever popular Dr Martens.*

constant emphasis on quality materials, with strict criteria applied throughout the buying process. Close working partnerships have been forged with the very best tanneries, and only the very best upper materials are considered; 'investing in the best to achieve the best' is a by-word at Griggs.

Although outwardly R Griggs and Co today, with factories scattered over Northamptonshire, Leicestershire, Warwickshire and Somerset and a global workforce of nearly 4,000, might bear little resemblance to the small-scale venture started in Wollaston almost a century ago, it is reassuring to discover that there has been no fundamental change in the outlook or the ethos of the company. It is still a privately-owned family firm and determined to remain so; and it is still a firm believer in the value of quality, comfort and durability. With the sole now made of an oil-based PVC granular compound resistant to oil, fat, acid, petrol and alkali, moulded into a carefully developed slip-limiting pattern and attached to the upper with invisible Goodyear stitching, Doc Marten's are produced at a rate of over a million a month. A piecework system is in operation at its factories which is popular with the employees because it permits very high earnings. Dr Martens are exported in quantity to Scandinavia, Japan, Canada, Italy, France and the USA; export sales rose from 0.3% in 1960 to 14.8% in 1990, and the company received the Queen's Award for Export in 1993 and again in 1997. In Great Britain, Docs are sold in shoe shops, multiple retailers,

Top: *The Clothes Show Live at the NEC in Birmingham.*
Right: *Providing excellent quality shoes with highly proficient equipment.*

department stores and through traditional safety footwear distributors. Griggs also owns the six-storey Dept Store in London's Covent Garden and other similar concept stores in various parts of the world; the prestigious retail site in Covent Garden was the company's first ever retail outlet, and has become established as one of London's best-known footwear and accessory outlets, attracting a huge number of customers from all walks of life.

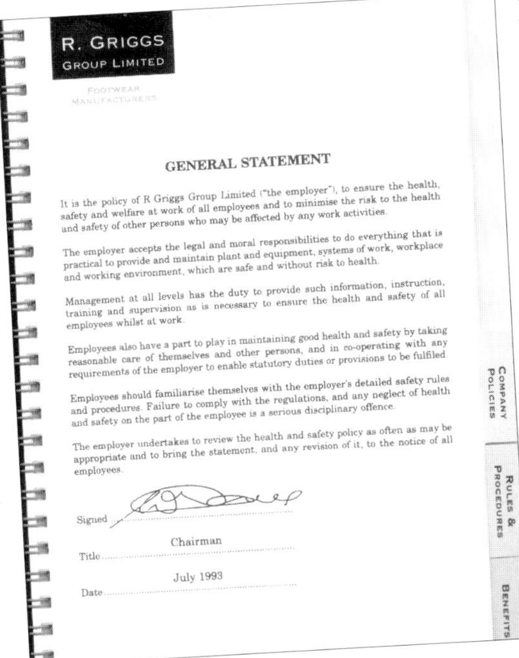

R. GRIGGS
GROUP LIMITED
FOOTWEAR MANUFACTURERS

GENERAL STATEMENT

It is the policy of R Griggs Group Limited ("the employer"), to ensure the health, safety and welfare at work of all employees and to minimise the risk to the health and safety of other persons who may be affected by any work activities.

The employer accepts the legal and moral responsibilities to do everything that is practical to provide and maintain plant and equipment, systems of work, workplace and working environment, which are safe and without risk to health.

Management at all levels has the duty to provide such information, instruction, training and supervision as is necessary to ensure the health and safety of all employees whilst at work.

Employees also have a part to play in maintaining good health and safety by taking reasonable care of themselves and other persons, and in co-operating with any requirements of the employer to enable statutory duties or provisions to be fulfiled.

Employees should familiarise themselves with the employer's detailed safety rules and procedures. Failure to comply with the regulations, and any neglect of health and safety on the part of the employee is a serious disciplinary offence.

The employer undertakes to review the health and safety policy as often as may be appropriate and to bring the statement, and any revision of it, to the notice of all employees.

Signed ....

Title Chairman

Date July 1993

COMPANY POLICIES | RULES & PROCEDURES | BENEFITS

Dr Martens footwear is popular with all types of people; London Underground and the Post Office are major customers in the UK, and Dr Martens are worn by policemen, punks, bankers, nurses, rock stars, industrial workers, teenagers, students and children; by men and women in search of comfort; and by affluent, image-conscious young men and women from all backgrounds in search of stylish street fashion.

Recognising that it was above all the youth market which helped launch Doc Marten's in the 60s and which has helped maintain its high profile, the company has established an on-going programme of help and financial support across a variety of youth-related initiatives. To mark its 30th anniversary in 1990, the company donated £250,000 to The Prince's Youth Business Trust, and has subsequently maintained its support of this organisation, also sponsoring such events as the catwalk displays at the Clothes Show Live, the PYBT Trade Fair at the International Autumn Fair, and the annual Battle of the Bands which offers aspiring and talented musicians from all over the country a performance platform and the chance of a recording contract.

Top: *An aerial view of R Griggs & Co's factory as it is today.*
Above: *A page from the current company handbook.*

Griggs also provides assistance for performers and is generous in its sponsorship of theatres, a musical dance company and a multi-racial band, and sponsors a number of festivals encompassing a variety of art forms. A range of sporting organisations including the Rushden & Diamonds Football Club, Dr Martens Football League, Northamptonshire County Cricket Club, Northampton Basketball Club and West Ham United Football Club's Football in the Community have benefited immensely from support from the Company; and national and local charities, local clubs, societies, schools and hospital also receive generous funding.

Now headed by Max and Stephen Grigg, Bill's son and grandson respectively, the Company is vigorously committed to maintaining its success in manufacturing Dr Martens and its tradition of involvement in the community, both locally and nationally - looking after the soul, as well as the

Top left: *The company's own outlet for loyal customers.* ***Top right:*** *The directors Max and Stephen Griggs.* ***Below:*** *The Diamond Centre is closely linked with the Group by Mr Max Griggs being the Chairman of the club.*

The core in the apple

It was the late 1960s, and described at the time as 'an apple without a core', Northampton lacked the attraction of the major shopping facilities enjoyed by nearby towns. Moreover, in 1968 the town had been officially designated as a New Town, and was nominated for significant expansion to help cope with London's overspill. An increase in population from 130,000 to 230,000 was expected, though the figure was later scaled down to 180,000. Even so, the town centre facilities that already existed were quite inadequate to meet the demands of the expected huge increase in population.

Northampton County Borough Council swung into action to carry out a number of major redevelopments, one of which was the proposed new Grosvenor Shopping Centre. Five acres adjoining Abington Street and the Market Square were allocated to the scheme which was eventually to regenerate the very heart of the town. The project was given into the hands of Grosvenor Estate Commercial Development Ltd, who had an enviable reputation as landowners in areas such as Mayfair and Belgravia. Their expertise in redevelopment work - including similar extensive undercover shopping centres - reached across the

country and overseas to Canada, Australia and other parts of the world. Grosvenor worked on the scheme in conjunction with the Post Office Pension Fund, who had in the past made significant investments in shopping developments in Corby, Stockton on Tees and Milton Keynes.

The initial task was to establish the eventual cost and viability of the project, and in-depth studies were carried out by Gleeds Quantity Surveyors. Numerous schemes were devised and costed; many were rejected, others were modified. At last the final design was arrived at and agreed. A list of contractors was compiled and invited to submit tenders to carry out the work.The contract for the building works was awarded to Wimpeys in April 1972, and they quickly began to clear the site earmarked for the new Centre.

The undertaking began with the demolition of the existing buildings, some of which were still occupied at the time, and with the clearing of two roads that were still in use across the site when work commenced. The site also contained the remains of an old Friary which was at the time being explored by archaeologists. The entire operation needed careful coordination in order to give consideration to the occupiers and archaeologists, and the work was accordingly phased over five months.

The site was eventually cleared and an incredible 80,000 cubic metres of earth were removed to make way for the foundations. Six tower cranes up to 150ft tall transported concrete to every part of the five acre site. As the new shopping centre grew, a small team of local stonemasons was engaged in the placing of hand-made facing bricks on certain of the elevations. All in all a total of 4,500 tons of reinforced concrete was used on the construction, and three million facing bricks were used on the external cladding of the building. The redevelopment plans included office space and car parking for a thousand cars as well as the

Above: *An archaelogical dig which took place on the site in the 1970s.*
Left: *Parade House, Market Square as it was 1880.*

enclosed two-tier shopping malls. In addition to the access staircases that link the malls, five passenger lifts were provided to serve the malls and car park above.

With the continuing safety of the public in mind, the Centre was designed in consultation with the Northamptonshire Fire Service's Fire Prevention Officer, and many safety features were incorporated into the design. A zoned fire alarm system was installed throughout the Centre, and an extensive sprinkler system, served by a large water storage tank housed in the car park entry ramp drum, formed a major part of the fire prevention arrangements. Each zone was individually relayed back to a panel situated in Management Control on the Service Deck. In turn this panel was designed to relay signals to the Fire Service headquarters, pinpointing an incident and even advising the Service which zone or entry point they should use in order to minimise delays.

Above: *Work began on the site in the summer of 1972.*

Smoke detectors were positioned in each of the exhaust air plants to give early warning of any problems, and hose reels and fire hydrants were also installed around the Centre.

Should there be a power cut at any time, the Centre's automatic diesel generator was designed to immediately kick in to provide 50 percent emergency lighting in all the pedestrian areas, and would also provide emergency power to ventilation plants and certain lifts. An air conditioning system was built into the design, to deliver around 50,000 cubic feet of fresh air every minute throughout the building, creating a controlled environment where shoppers would be able to browse in comfort around their favourite stores.

Creating a shopping complex that was not only a useful facility, with access by pedestrian walkway directly from the bus station, but was at the same time attractive and comfortable to the shopping public was essential to the whole concept of adding life and sparkle to the town centre. Spaciousness without monotony was the aim of the architects Stone Toms and Partners, and the resulting generously wide and stylishly designed shopping malls with simple finishes, large floor tiles, and a marble finish to walls and columns were a tribute to their expertise. Column-free areas were provided at lower mall level. The clever variation in ceiling height throughout the building added to the feeling of depth and space, while the intensity of lighting in the malls, installed in recessed fittings, was kept to an intentionally low level to emphasise the individual lighting given out by each of the shop units.

On the upper mall Stone Toms designed The Friary, giving it vaulted ceilings, quarry tile flooring and effective concealed fluorescent lighting that lent a cloister-like feeling to the area. Positioned approximately above the excavated site of the old Greyfriars Monastery, The Friary was meant to ensure that this part of the town's rich history, excavated by archaeologists in 1970, would not be forgotten. The Friary became an attractive setting for the group of small shops set around an open cafe in the centre.

The building fronted on to one of the most impressive market squares in the country, so the facade itself required careful planning to ensure that it was built in sympathy with the rest of Market Square. When it came to planning the exterior, the Percy Thomas Partnership was brought in to assist Stone Toms in designing the Market Square frontage. The long history of the square goes back to Medieval times, and everyone involved in the planning

Above: *The Friary under construction.*

recognised the importance of retaining the character of this unique and distinctive square while at the same time regenerating the area.

It was quite a challenge. In order to achieve architectural harmony the rest of the buildings in the square had to be taken into consideration, and the architects carefully considered their heights and widths, roof profiles, window proportions and facing materials. Rebuilding of the sixteenth-century Welsh House, situated at the north-east corner of the square, formed an important part of the new development.

Welsh House had for a long time been in very poor structural condition and had originally been earmarked for demolition. Happily, the authorities decided to retain and reconstruct the ancient building, retaining its original architectural character. The superbly recreated building was eventually occupied by Church's China Stores. Church's, probably the best known family business in Northampton, moved into the town in 1858.

THE EXCITING AND INNOVATIVE SHOPPING CENTRE WAS BUILT TO A DESIGN THAT WAS STILL UNUSUAL WHEN IT WAS OPENED TO THE PUBLIC

The exciting and innovative shopping centre, built to a design that was still unusual when it was opened to the shopping public, was the combined result of all the painstaking planning of the numerous bodies involved in its conception, design and construction. The resulting facility is a credit to their various talents and expertise. The stylish Grosvenor Centre quickly became a source of

Above: *The interior as it was in the late 1970s.*

pride and pleasure in the town - and remains so today.

The Centre's great attraction was that almost anything could be bought under one roof, and when it was opened stores such as Church's, Habitat, Waring and Gillow, Miss Selfridge, Boots, Sainsbury's, W H Smith, Saxone, Dixons and Beatties - to name only a few - provided people with a wide choice of goods from food to fashions and from photography to flowers.

Over the years the Grosvenor Centre acquired its own unique character, becoming a popular focal point where friends could meet and have a cup of coffee or something more substantial before doing the rounds of a huge choice of exciting shops and stores that range from large chain stores to small specialist retailers. Today it is so much a part of the town that shoppers can scarcely imagine life without the Grosvenor Centre, which has truly become the core in the apple.

Today, further plans are afoot for the Centre's future. When Barclaycard vacated 150,000 square feet of office space in Greyfriars House in 1997 various options were discussed. Few business tenants were interested in moving in, and a scheme to convert the offices into more than 100 flats was considered and judged to be extremely difficult to bring about. The most likely option discussed was that of conversion to retail use, and property developers began discussing plans with Northampton Borough Council to expand the shopping facilities even further.

At the end of the 1990s Grosvenor Shopping Centre faces the next millennium with confidence, certain that whatever developments take place over the coming months and years, the Centre is assured of a future as exciting and innovative as its past.

£80million

That's the asking price as Grosvenor Centre is put up for sale by current owners

Ambitious expansion plans could see town centre shopping complex double in size

__Above:__ An article that appeared in the local newspaper when the centre was offered for sale. __Top:__ The Market Square facade.

A great way to shop 'til you drop

When application was made back in January 1972 for planning permission to turn an area of undeveloped wasteland into a new shopping centre, few could have visualised the eventual outcome - a lively, bustling facility with an incredible 255,175 square feet of climatically controlled shopping area, and parking space, both outdoor and undercover, for more than 1,000 vehicles. Six months after the application was made the go-ahead was given by the Secretary of State for the Environment, and during the Autumn, with Mr Gordon Redfern in charge of the centre's design, work on Phase 1 of the Weston Favell Shopping Centre got underway.

When the centre was opened on 29th October 1974 by Baroness Evelyn Sharp the building still wore an air of unfinished bareness - at least from the outside, where building work was still going on. Inside, it was a different story. Pleasantly light and cheerful, the spacious enclosed shopping area immediately put the VIPs attending the opening ceremony at their ease. Baroness Sharp, who had been Permanent Secretary of the Ministry of Housing and Development, confessed in her speech that initially she had had some doubts about how well the Development Corporation and the Borough Council would work closely together on the project; the reality, however, had far exceeded her hopes. Dr John Weston, General Manager of the Northampton Development Corporation, was forced to attend the ceremony in a wheelchair. An unfortunate accident while on holiday in the Lake District had resulted in a broken leg - and presented him with a golden opportunity to put the centre's wheelchair ramps to the test!

The centre was home to a huge Tesco superstore, by far the Tesco group's largest development, exceeding by 22,000 square feet the previous largest, in Stevenage. The group's firm declaration was to make this branch of Tesco's one of the most successful in the world. Lines of shopping trolleys, as yet unused, waited inside the doors for the store's first shoppers. The trolleys cost around £20 each - a daunting sum of money 25 years ago.

The invention of the £1 slot to ensure the safe return of shopping trolleys was still some way in the future.

Shoppers were immediately at ease with the town's new shopping centre. The idea of shopping in a facility that was under cover and therefore sheltered from cold winds and driving rain held great appeal. The temperature-controlled environment that was snugly comfortable in the howling winds of winter was also a cool refuge from the hot sun of summer. The upper shopping mall was built with a high barrel-vaulted ceiling that allowed natural light to filter through along

***Right:** Construction work began on the Weston Favell Shopping Centre in June 1972.*

its 180 metre length, giving the impression of browsing in an old traditional shopping arcade. The arcaded mall played its own part in making the new Weston Favell Centre popular with the majority of Northampton's shopping public. A lower shopping mall ran alongside the entire length of the undercover parking facilities.
As well as the huge number of shops of every kind, including Boots and W H Smith (who in the late 1990s are still there), the centre offered the benefits of two major supermarkets, with Supacentre being housed there as well as the large Tesco store. There was little need for shoppers to go elsewhere, as linked by a series of ramps, escalators, autowalks and lifts, around fifty shops and stores made sure that most if not all of their needs could be supplied under one roof. Ladies' fashions, menswear, knitting wools, haberdashery and supplies for the handicraft enthusiast, books, gifts, toiletries and medication - all were there to offer their tempting wares to the buyer. And when shoppers had 'shopped till they dropped' they could take their weary feet into the nearest coffee shop to snatch a quick cuppa or enjoy a more substantial meal; both supermarkets offered cafeterias as part of their service. The centre also had other services such as banks, building societies, a post office and a library on the premises, while the Emmanuel Church catered for the spiritual needs of the people - as it still does today.
In 1979, five years after its opening, plans were drawn up to add a bazaar to the Weston Favell Shopping Centre. Fearing, however, that this would have an adverse effect on the market in the town céntre, the new development was turned down by Northampton Borough Council.
Two years later the wedding of Prince Charles and the Lady Diana Spencer gave Centre Manager Victor Bravington and his team an opportunity to demonstrate Northampton's loyalty. They rose to the challenge and went to town on the decorations, planning various promotions and activities to mark the romantic occasion, which was to end with a funfair on the Pyramid car park. Colourful bunting and patriotic flags were strung across the length of the mall, and banners and huge photographs of the royal couple

Above: *The shopping centre with the suburbs of Northampton behind in a picture dating from 1977.*

hung from the vaulted ceiling. The shy young Princess Diana and her Prince Charming had stolen the hearts of the people, and there was no shadow then of the tragic events to come to mar the town's celebrations. An attraction with a difference was added to the Weston Favell Centre in 1982, when a giant aquarium was placed in the car park. The fish on show turned out to be not the usual kind of tropical fish one might expect to see in an aquarium, but sharks - four of them! The tank contained not only sharks, but a girl to ride on them; Miss Bette Hasse, a German marine biologist, performed with the sharks until she had to return to Germany to care for a sick shark. Her place was then taken by twenty-year-old Australian Colette Hayman, who took risks with these Jaws lookalikes that very few young girls would relish. Colette would enter the tank every day to give a performance - and confessed to enjoying sending shudders of horror through her

Above: *The Mall at the Weston Favell Centre in readiness for the wedding of Lady Diana Spencer and Prince Charles in July 1981.*

shows, a children's playland and a walking, talking robot to provide entertainment for the children (and their parents?). During the birthday week live shows were broadcast from the shopping centre by Radio Northampton and Hereward Radio.

The years between 1984 and 1998 have seen a number of changes of ownership, with Tesco British Land Property Partnership taking over in September 1997. The following April Nick Smith was appointed Centre Manager.

In the 24 years that have passed since the opening of Weston Favell Shopping Centre, the centre has gone from strength to strength, with various refurbishments taking place and the North Square kiosks being added. Such a development, of course, does not stand still for long, and various expansions to the Tesco superstore and to the centre itself are at present being whispered of. Whatever improvements are in the wind, the shoppers of Northampton are sure to remain happy with the shopping centre that has served them well from the day of its opening so long ago; and look forward to the silver anniversary celebrations in 1999.

audience when she rode the nurse shark right up to the glass window! The lemon sharks, however, were a different story. Colette would never touch their rough skin because of the risk of her bleeding from a scratch. Readers familiar with the film 'Jaws' will appreciate what that could lead to! After five minutes or so the sharks would get restless and begin to circle the girl; that was when Colette would call time on her dangerous stunt. Londoner Janette Flook, aged nineteen, would also perform with the sharks.

In 1984 Capital and Counties Shopping Centres took over the ownership of the centre, and Mr Robert Baldry became Centre Manager. The same year saw the celebration of Weston Favell's 10th Anniversary, and to celebrate the management staged Punch and Judy

Weston Favell Shopping Centre acknowledge the loan of the photographs by The Chronicle and Echo.

Above: *This picture from 1982 shows a shark display at the centre which involved the use of a giant aquarium.*
Top: *The centre today.*

Building for the future

'When you've been building homes for more than 90 years, you learn a lot...' The bold statement conspicuously placed inside the front cover of the Wilcon Homes brochure for 1998 speaks volumes about the company's long experience and expertise in home building.

It all started back in 1905, when a young Englishman Thomas Wilson returned home after spending ten years in America. A shoemaker by trade, Thomas had decided to seek his fortune in the New World at the end of the 19th century. Along with thousands of other Britons he emigrated to the States, working his passage across. In New England he tried a variety of jobs that led him into the building trade and sparked off a love of building that was to eventually become part of the industry's history. After a decade spent in New England he returned to his native Northampton, bringing with him his young bride, Elizabeth Connolly.

Before long Thomas Wilson had converted an old windmill into an unusual and comfortable home for himself and Elizabeth. Their son Connolly Thomas was born there during the same year. Thomas was soon occupied in constructing his first house, 'Hillcrest', which he built for his brother-in-law. The house, bearing the date 1905, still stands today. Thomas soon built up a reputation in Northampton for the quality of his work, and his hand-truck, with his name in copper-plate script on the side, became a familiar sight around the town. When the Northampton Tramway decided to extend its services and add an extension to the St James Tram Depot, it was Thomas Wilson who was given the contract - the first of a number for the tramway.

In 1927 Thomas Wilson became the proud owner of a second hand Model T Ford lorry, purchased for £15 - his first step into mechanisation! That same year he built himself a new house in the village of Gayton, erecting his own brickworks on an adjoining field. Four years later the company bought their first new lorry and painted it in the handsome brown and cream Wilson livery. They were really on their way.
Other important contracts followed. They won the

***Above:** Thomas Wilson with his wife in retirement at Gayton. **Left:** Thomas Wilson's windmill home. The windmill was used as the company symbol throughout the 1920s and 30s. **Below:** The original Ford Model T and Lloyd Labrum who joined the company in 1924 and retired in the late 1970s.*

contract from Northampton Corporation to build the new slipper baths in Spencer Bridge Road, described by the Mayor of Northampton at the official opening of the baths in 1928 as 'A boon for the working classes'.

In 1930 Thomas's son Connolly joined the business which was then registered as T Wilson & Son Ltd, with offices in Regent Street and workshops in Broad Street. Con, as the young man was affectionately known, began to steer the company into further growth and development. The government's policy of home-building during the 1930s helped the expansion. Wilson's 'Villa Residences' and their £550 three-bedroom 'Sunshine Villas', described as 'The labour saving sensation of the year', were built in and around Northampton, and a development of bungalows was constructed at Overstone and Sywell.

Con Wilson took the decision to form a property company, Newilton Ltd, to build a block of flats in Derngate, Northampton. The one and two-bedroom flats, called Bedford Mansions, each had central heating, hot water and a lock-up garage, and the building boasted an attractive roof garden and a resident caretaker.

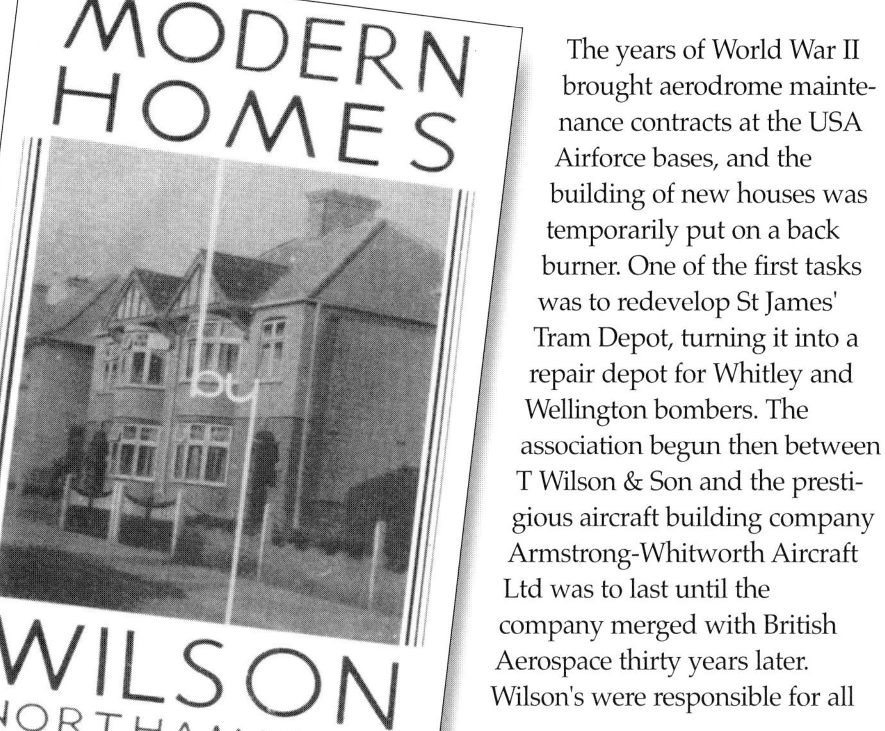

The years of World War II brought aerodrome maintenance contracts at the USA Airforce bases, and the building of new houses was temporarily put on a back burner. One of the first tasks was to redevelop St James' Tram Depot, turning it into a repair depot for Whitley and Wellington bombers. The association begun then between T Wilson & Son and the prestigious aircraft building company Armstrong-Whitworth Aircraft Ltd was to last until the company merged with British Aerospace thirty years later. Wilson's were responsible for all

Left: *An advertisement from the 1930s for one of the company's 'Tudor style villas'.* ***Below:*** *67 Sheep Street, to where the company moved when the Regent Street premises proved too small.*

building and repairs at the USAAF bases at Grafton Underwood, Chelveston and Poddington, which on occasions meant filling in craters left by crashed planes. C T Wilson's sons Con and Lynn, who in later years both joined him in the business, would often accompany their father on his visits to the bases and come away with their pockets filled with American candy bars - a real treat in wartime Britain. Lynn Wilson is today the Chairman of Wilcon Homes.

After the war it was 'business as usual' and in 1947 a development of 96 houses was sold to the Corporation. Throughout the post-war years Wilson's continued to expand, building an industrial estate on Weedon Road and constructing both private and corporation housing estates. During the 1950's building boom Wilson's were building over 200 homes per year for Northampton Corporation. Factories and laboratories for Plessey Ltd followed. The company's Golden Jubilee Year of 1955 saw C T Wilson honoured with the OBE for his outstanding services to the building industry, and he received the decoration from the Queen at Buckingham Palace.

That same year, while driving home from Coventry, Con Wilson passed a board advertising building plots for sale in Rugby. On impulse he turned his car around, drove into Rugby to investigate - and came away the owner of a number of plots. That was the start of the company's development into Rugby, where around a thousand homes were built over the next 25 years. Expansion of the company during the 1950s meant that more space was needed. In 1957 the old joinery works in Broad Street were converted into offices, and a new works built on the Weedon Road Industrial Estate. The 1960s saw the company extending eastwards into Peterborough. A key move in 1965 brought all the Wilson companies together into a single holding company with C T Wilson as chairman, and a year later Wilson (Connolly) Holdings Ltd became a public quoted company. In 1970 Con Wilson, known for many years simply as the 'Gov'nor' died - a sad loss to the company that had benefited from his input since 1930.

The appointment of enthusiastic young executives, including Michael Robinson, coupled with the improving economic situation of the early 1970s, helped Wilson Connolly spread its wings into new areas of the country, appointing Regional and Area Managers with a wealth of experience at their fingertips. The luxury housing development at Cedar Hythe, Chapel Brampton, won the Award for Good Design in Housing in 1974, setting a further seal on the company's achievements. Two years later saw Wilson Connolly celebrate its tenth birthday as a public company; that same year, 1976, the turnover was in excess of £12m. More than a thousand homes were being built every year on fifty different sites between Southampton and Humberside. Space was once more found to be at a premium, so the old offices were demolished and the site redeveloped, and a new block of offices was built on the Moulton Park Estate.

Below: *A typical waterfront development.*

5 bedroom family house

The Group has continually sought to be at the forefront of new building techniques and environmental concerns, using derelict sites to build stylish housing, transforming storm water lagoons into tasteful waterside developments and retaining established trees on building land. Cotswold stone, flint walls, patterned brickwork, and the use of local materials and styles make each development full of character and attractive to the eye.

Maisonettes & town houses

Today, with more than 4,000 families moving into a Wilcon home every year, the company is one of the most successful and respected house builders in the country, and the team believe that it is Wilson Connolly's commitment to quality that has been the key to their success. Beginning with the choosing of a location where people would want to live, the company is involved at every step in designing comfortable and attractive homes that reflect the changing tastes of customers, and at the end of the day they feel that they can step back and take genuine pride in their achievements.

5 bedroom family house

Wilcon in conjunction with Integer built a concept house for the new millennium to feature in a six programme series of the BBC's Dream House programme.

The BBC's Dream House

Designed to be eco-friendly and as sustainable as possible the home incorporates pioneering construction techniques, state-of-the-art technologies in leisure, entertainment, comfort, security, IT, communications and safety as well as energy management, water conservation and other environmental initiatives.

5 bedroom family house

As we enter the new millennium, Wilson Connolly, with around 3,000 shareholders, a turnover of circa £400million, an operation that is spread across the country and completing around 5,000 new homes per annum, has established itself as one of the leaders of the British Housebuilding Industry - a record of which Thomas Wilson would have been

Right: *Lynn Wilson - Chairman.*

The family firm that makes sure local industry gets what it needs

In the early 1930s, Frederick George Metcalfe's grandfather, the local carrier, made a decision which was to be of major future benefit not only to Frederick's family but to the businesses of Northampton and the surrounding areas: he decided to share out his savings, and gave £75 to each of his three grandchildren. Frederick was determined that his own £75 share would be put to the best possible use, and he made careful plans for it: £25 was earmarked for one month's rent on a warehouse with a house attached at 67 Military Road, and for his living expenses during that period; £25 was handed over to Earl Spencer's agent at Althorp in exchange for a second hand, fabric bodied Austin 7; and the remaining £25 was to be set aside to pay suppliers who insisted on cash with order. Frederick had decided to set himself up in the distribution trade.

Prior to this, Frederick had served an apprenticeship with an ironmonger in Bedford before joining up to serve during the first world war. After the war, on his return from service in France, he had taken a job as a representative in the mill furnishing department of the well-know local company A Bell & Co Ltd, Ironmongers, who were based in Gold Street, Northampton, and who supplied belting and pulleys, nuts and bolts, pipes and fittings, and hand tools to local factories and tanneries. Frederick had therefore learned first-hand the requirements of local businesses, and his new venture defied the Great Depression and was an immediate success. By 1936 Frederick, now accompanied by his wife Dorothea and son John, had moved to a larger warehouse, which again had a house attached, at 74 Earl Street. Here the company managed to survive the difficult trading conditions of the second world war, a period which was very restrictive to enterprise and imposed severe controls on the distributive trade. Frederick's customers were still mostly local leather tanneries, boot and shoe factories, and the maintenance engineers who serviced such diverse trades as the dairies, breweries and millers.

Below: *Fred Metcalfe outside the Earl Street premises in 1948.*

Frederick's son John joined his father in the business in 1945, acting, amongst other things, as delivery boy; the company had no motor vehicle, and John still remembers the challenges involved in delivering galvanised steel sheets and 21ft lengths of pipe on his pushbike. In due course, however, John was called up for National Service, and when his father died in 1951 he was at first unsure whether to return to Northampton carry on the family business, or whether to pursue his career in the Army. Encouraged by his mother, he chose to settle down at Earl Street, and the following year he married Daphne, to whom the firm is indebted for her hard work and support over the years.

The years which followed saw a shift in the pattern of industry in Northampton and the surrounding area; the numerous leatherworks and shoe manufacturers which had previously formed the main focus of the area's manufacturing activity were now being replaced by new, larger factories and engineering works. Metcalfe's continued to sell industrial ironmongery but also diversified into transmission and steam heating equipment which they supplied to factory maintenance crews and to the heating and ventilation engineers who were involved in fitting out the new factories; they also became involved in engineering production tools, from twist drills and milling cutters to lathes. As the business built up John needed extra help, and he recruited a 17 year old school leaver, Anthony Stokes, who now manages the Northampton branch, and a sales rep. Janitorial products were introduced to the company's stocklist, with Metcalfe's becoming Kimberly Clark's first franchised distributor, and, encouraged by the rapid success of Kimwipes and other such products which were a new departure for them, the company became increasingly adventurous in the range of products it supplied. Metcalfe's was the first engineers' merchant to stock Swarfega, which had previously been sold only through the motor trade's accessory outlets or direct to the big factories. It was also the first to supply Rocol, at a time when the industry at large was very suspicious of advanced lubrication techniques. Other products for which the company has acted as agents include the Erecto slotted angle racking system, Revvo industrial castors, imports from Holo-Krome, Mitutoyo, Sandvik, Ceka, and an American product 'Rustoleum', an industrial anti-rust system.

As a result of this continued wide diversification in products and the increased turnover which resulted, the company again began to outgrow its

Above: *Inside the well stocked counter and showroom area.* ***Below:*** *The Metcalfe family today. Front: Daphne and John Metcalfe. Back: Sarah, Ian and Andrew.*

premises; by the late 1960s more room had become an absolute necessity and the firm moved to Dunster Street, where expansion continued. The opening of the motorway network brought further changes to the pattern of business; new businesses, though not all of them manufacturers, were encouraged into Northampton, whilst at the same time the motorways opened the way for competition from other industrial distributors further afield. In response to the new trading conditions, Metcalfe's began to extend their own territory. A second branch was opened in East Dereham, Norfolk, and continued trading until 1986, and a third branch opened in Milton Keynes in 1982. The Milton Keynes branch is managed by Brian Curtis. Further branches were opened: in Aylesbury, under the management of David Smart and in Oxford, where the manager is Terry Wickens.

In 1982 F G Metcalfe and Sons Limited celebrated its golden jubilee in 1982, and to mark the occasion it sponsored a match at the Weedon Road football ground between the 'Saints', Northampton Football Club, and Cambridge University.

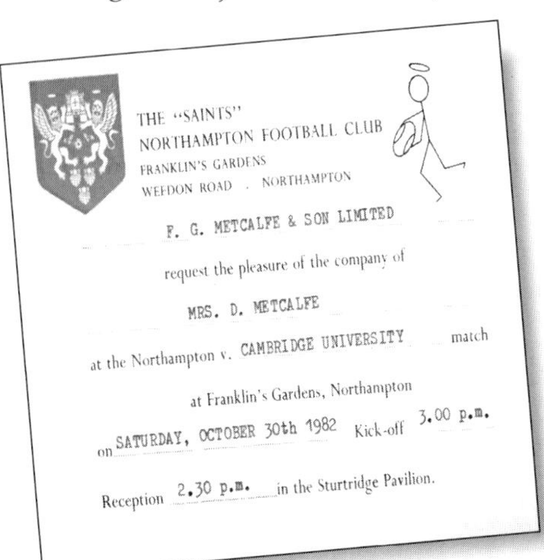
THE "SAINTS"
NORTHAMPTON FOOTBALL CLUB
FRANKLIN'S GARDENS
WEEDON ROAD . NORTHAMPTON

F. G. METCALFE & SON LIMITED

request the pleasure of the company of

MRS. D. METCALFE

at the Northampton v. CAMBRIDGE UNIVERSITY match

at Franklin's Gardens, Northampton

on SATURDAY, OCTOBER 30th 1982 Kick-off 3.00 p.m.

Reception 2.30 p.m. in the Sturtridge Pavilion.

Andrew Metcalfe took over the task of running the Company in 1990 and was appointed Managing Director, with his brother Ian, as Director responsible for transport (A most important element in any distribution organisation). They became the third generation to serve other industries in their branch areas. The two brothers were shortly joined by their sister Sarah Hobbs, who now takes her part in helping the business to run smoothly. By this time the company's main offices had moved from Dunster Street to St James Mill Road, which gave them accommodation of 21,500 square feet on a freehold one-acre site and computers had been introduced; and John's two sons Ian and Andrew had begun to learn about the business.

The firm's high standards of service gained recognition in 1998 when F G Metcalfe won three out of the seven categories at the annual industry awards organised by Engineering Distributor magazine. John Metcalfe received the prestigious Distributor of the Year Award, Andrew Metcalfe received the Marketing and Presentation Award and David Smart the Individual Award. And tributes to the firm continued the following day when Metcalfe's was highly commended in the Cleaning and Hygiene Suppliers Association Distributor Service Excellence Awards.

A well-planned and efficient administration system has contributed to the success of the company over the years. Having been one of the

***Above:** The Office Block at St James Mill Road with the warehouse in the background - 1995.*

first in the industry to computerise, the system has been constantly updated as technology has progressed. Structurally, the firm is divided into seven divisions, with more planned for the future: the current divisions are fasteners, pipeline, janitorial, workwear, welding, coatings and general line. It has its own in-house manufacturing facilities for Carbide Cutting Tools which are marketed under the registered Tradename 'Rapier'. Also on the premises is a laundry to cater for its rapidly expanding workwear supply and overall laundering clientele. In addition there is machinery on site for cutting and threading tube to customer's special requirements. Paint mixing equipment is on hand to cater for every shade of coating a customer may require in his factory or outside.

From the earliest days of the business, turnover has been built up on the tradition of service and sense of duty towards the customer which remains a priority today. Today, all major factories in Metcalfe's areas hold accounts with the firm, and, with a regular client base of some 5,000 customers who represent a cross-section of local industry such as engineers and food and drink manufacturers, Metcalfe's is firmly established as a major industrial distributor. Specialist staff are employed to assimilate and evaluate the latest innovations and to provide technical advice and assistance to customers. Many of the employees have long experience of the business, having been with the company for many years; this has helped the company to successfully maintain, throughout its development and growth, the atmosphere of the family business, and customers appreciate the personal attention and the courtesy, commitment and experience of the staff.

The firm's recent move to new premises in Studland Road will permit its impressive range of stock to be expanded still further. The company sees customer satisfaction as the key to its success, and the means achieving its goal of maximising its share of the industrial distribution market within Northamptonshire, Buckinghamshire and Oxfordshire. And Metcalfe's many satisfied customers will be quick to agree that the £75 which Frederick George Metcalfe was given by his grandfather in 1932 could not have been put to better use.

Above: *John Metcalfe (Chairman) receives the 1997 Engineering Distributor of the Year Award.* ***Below:*** *View of the firm's present Head Office premises in Studland Road.*

Pioneers in Family Health Care

The Northamptonshire and District Hospitals Guild can trace its origin to funds raised by the Order of Forresters to assist the family of Benjamin Smith, fireworks maker, in July 1874 following a disastrous explosion at his house. The brethren of his order had raised the considerable sum of £51-4s-6d (£51.22p) by holding a Fete and Gala. As the entire family died these funds were donated to the Northampton Infirmary.

Inspired by this tragic event an enthusiastic public meeting at the Town Hall on 23 February 1875 carried unanimously the proposal ."Seeing the many and continually increasing demands made upon the charity of the Northampton General Infirmary and the estimation in which that institution is held, it is desirable that a Hospital Sunday Movement be inaugurated in the Town, whereby the working classes may be enabled to subscribe to that excellent institution by which so many of the are benefited." The collections which immediately followed, in factories, chapels and churches, raised £873 donated to the hospital in an era when hospitals were poorly funded by a mixture of ancient beneficiary investments, private donations and subscriptions from the public of all classes.

Nineteenth century medical care, like so many old parish based services, had failed to keep up with the enormous demand generated by the uncontrolled growth of industrial towns. It was not until the 1870s that volunteer administrators, drawn from the local gentry and other public spirited individuals, were replaced on any appreciable scale, at both county and town council levels, by salaried officials paid from the rates. In those days working people

gained admission to their nearest hospital on the strength of a letter of recommendation from their employer who, in turn, was responsible for administering the hospital insurance payments collected from his employees. One such employer in 1904 was Mr F G Adnitt, then Chairman of the Hospital Committee, whose successful drapery shop is now part of the Debenham's chain.

When the world changed in 1914 Mr J Gribble JP set up the Allied War Fund with the twofold purpose of aiding war funds and topping up local charities. People maintained weekly contributions which raised £40,000 in four years of which almost £17,322 went to local charities in an age when average wages were around £2 a week. From this was developed the Northamptonshire Hospital and Convalescent Fund in 1919, to assist the enormous body of war wounded men in their slow return to health; later it was called the Gribble Fund after its founder.

The work done by the Hospital Week Committee was a vital source of money to the General Hospital, formerly the Infirmary. During their Jubilee year two new operating theatres were funded by a special appeal which proved that local people valued their local hospital to the extent of funding extensions and improvements themselves.

In the 1920s local government took on responsibility for housing the sick poor in what were known as 'Poor Law Hospitals', often established in former workhouses to the distress of the inmates. The Voluntary Hospitals, such as the Northamptonshire Infirmary, then specialised in short term medical and surgical cases where the poor obtained free treatment from

They turned out despite

CARNIVAL HERO[ES] OF THEM!

Shivering Queen sets example

HEROES they were called and heroes they were—the 2,000 gallant, but dripping people who last night braved the worst weather conditions for years in Northampton's annual Carnival parade.

A few did not turn up, but most did and they laughed at the weather. Girls in grass skirts and boys in swimming trunks ignored a steady downpour as the floats gathered for the judging at Midsummer Meadow. It must have been difficult to achieve the "carnival" spirit with dye from paper flowers and make-up running down their faces, and it must have been discouraging to see costumes which had taken hours to make becoming bedraggled in a few minutes.

COLOUR EVERYWHERE

DAMP, BUT UNDETERRED

Mayoress present prizes

Above: *A newspaper clipping from the 1964 Northampton Charity Gala.*
Top: *A 'Fancy Dress' competition from the same event.*
Facing page, top: *An early advertisement.*
Facing page, bottom: *The Carnival float on the streets of Northampton in 1963.*

Honorary GPs and surgeons who visited hospitals on a part time basis.

At the other end of the social scale were those in comfortable circumstances, able to pay for private treatment in hospitals and nursing homes. As always those in between these extremes were caught out by earning enough to lift them above receiving charitable help but not enough to pay privately. It was these families, the backbone of any community, for whom sickness often caused real hardship.

IN 1948 THE NATIONAL HEALTH SCHEME BROUGHT INTO REALITY THE DREAM OF HEALTHCARE FROM 'THE CRADLE TO THE GRAVE'

On 27 September 1932 the Hospitals Guild Scheme changed its character from a charity to being a medical insurance fund. Salaried workers able to pay an annual fee could benefit in the same way as wage earners making weekly contributions. The top earnings limit allowed for membership was £250 per annum at a time when junior officers in the forces and senior clerks got £150pa. Successful professional men earning £500pa were regarded as wealthy indeed while living in nurses were lucky to receive thirty shillings (£1.50) a week. The Almoner (Hospital Welfare Officer) appointed in 1938 noticed that hospital staff were no longer checking that patients had paid in to the diverse number of Funds which entitled them to treatment. Voluntary hospitals could not afford to spend limited funds on providing for those able to obtain goods and services elsewhere.

As a result of this discovery the General Hospital proposed that all the fund raising groups combine under the new name of the Hospitals Guild, which despite some opposition eventually came into being. Ten years later, in 1948, the National Health Scheme brought into reality the dream of health care 'from the cradle to the grave' paid for by taxation and accessible to all British citizens, and not a few foreigners too.

Below: *Current Chief Executive, John Michael and Chariman, Ken Briers congratulate Miss Doris Streeter and Mrs Brenda Dyer on their retirement in 1998 with over 110 years service between them.*

The Labour government of the time believed that there was no longer any need for the 400-odd local hospital subscription schemes throughout Britain whose buildings and invested funds they had absorbed into the new NHS. This takeover included Battle House on the Billing Road and all the money raised by local people for their hospital!
The strength of public feeling coupled with a realisation that even socialist ideals could not function without voluntary funding prompted the government to allow the old hospital contributary organisations to operate locally for the benefit of their members. Although the NDHG was allowed to work from Battle House for a period nothing in the way of property or investments were ever returned!

Subsequent removals via Portland Street to present premises in St Giles Street have been accompanied by increases in staff from an original one and a half to fourteen at HQ plus two sub-offices at Rushden and Wellingborough to cope with the modern demand for private medical insurance. The NDHG has long been a member of the British Hospitals Contributory Schemes Association founded in 1931 which continued to work after the foundation of the NHS with a membership of thirty four schemes.
Most of these member schemes have been serving their localities for over a century.

The renamed British Health Care Association sets standards for its members to attain and works as a pressure group to prevent legislation which might restrict the services offered to subscribers.

Throughout the UK there are three million people who invest in local health schemes, of whom over thirty thousand are in Northamptonshire.

The NDHG currently pays out benefits annually of £1.5M, which reflects the national picture of paying out to members in respect of medical treatment of all kinds, of which 'in-patient' claims were almost 30%. Grants for spectacles and dental treatment charges repay those wise subscribers who would otherwise be out of pocket when paying for goods not covered by the NHS. Maternity grants are of course a regular item in the NDHG accounts while Physiotherapy treatment is a rapidly growing newcomer where benefits are £1M paid out to cover sports injuries etc. to those members who, intent on keeping fit, occasionally strained themselves. Members referred by their GPs to expensive specialists and surgeons need have no fear of paying their fees when covered by NDHG. Long convalescence, once an enjoyable privilege of the few, has been reduced to the minimum needed to allow injured body parts time for rest and repair, even so the The Hospitals Guild can cover its members for that as well.

The well tried tradition of voluntary service to one's community is still of vital importance to the success of the Hospitals Guild. The hundred Village Groups are each staffed by between one and seven volunteers who collect subscriptions from their neighbours and organise the fundraising events which are so much a part of rural life. The NDHG, like all voluntary groups, is constantly in need of 'new blood' to replace those who retire or move away. The NHS, like some medical charities, receives, and relies upon, donations made by contributory schemes funded by members of local groups such as the NDHG. An inspection of any local hospital will show the wards, theatres and equipment funded by the public through their weekly or monthly membership contributions as in the past hundred years and more. On 1st January 1997 NDHG merged with Anglia Healthcare, a similar scheme based in Norwich, becoming Healthcare Insurance Alliance Ltd. Both Schemes continue to operate successfully from their existing premises.

Above: *Mr Raymond Dyer, who was Secretary of the Hospital Guild and died in 1988.*
Right: *Edwin Dyer (son of Raymond Dyer), Chief Executive of the Fund until his death in 1995.*

Beautiful bodies and smart models

Joseph Grose was both pioneer and master of the now almost-extinct craft of bespoke carriage-work. The son of a tailor, Joseph started work in the leather trade, and subsequently set up his own business as a currier and leather seller. Always a keen cyclist, he held speed records in Penny Farthing races and designed his own lightweight racing bicycle. Then, when the safety bicycle was invented, cycling became immensely popular. Joseph took a small shop at 21 St James's Road and set up as a cycle agent, also manufacturing a range of bicycle accessories. Many of these used leather, and some of them he patented, such as carriers, non-rattling patent leather mudguards, a leather toolbag which fitted within the cycle frame, and 'a new adjustable chain and chain wheel cover and lubricator for bicycles', patented in 1892 and consisting of a metal and leather cover which stopped the chain from catching in ladies' skirts, and, for good measure, lubricated it as it went round.

By 1897 Joseph Grose had shops in Coventry and London and a large workshop, formerly a theatre and concert hall, at 63 Gold Street, and he was a wealthy man - sufficiently wealthy to become the first automobile-owner in Northampton. He first drove through Northampton on his new three-wheeled Motette, designed by Leon Bolle, on Saturday 24 April 1897, greatly amazing the Saturday shoppers and finally skidding and spinning near the church, where the road surface was made of wooden blocks and had become slippery. That same year he set up as agent for The Coventry Motor Co. As well as selling vehicles, he began to build a range of vehicle bodies, and in February 1900 the firm sold Grose Gear Case Company and established itself as Grose Limited in premises in Pike Lane off Marefair. There, perhaps mindful of his skid by the church, Grose Non-Skid Tyres were manufactured; these were leather cases with rivetted steel studs, fitted round the tyre to give extra grip. Another invention was the Grose Non-Skid and Puncture Proof Tyre, which was more densely studded to give more protection from the many horseshoes-nails which littered the roads.

Above left: *Mr Grose and his family at the turn of the century.* ***Below:*** *The Grose premises with the workshops in the background in 1912.*

In the early days of cars, it was common for the larger, more expensive models to be delivered in chassis form, and the body custom-built to the wishes of the purchaser. Grose built bodywork individually designed for customers, and also carried out work for other well-established bodyworks. The company became deservedly famous for the many beautiful and luxurious bodies it constructed on chassis such as the Alvis Super Sports, the 20/70 Crossley sports-type chassis and other prestige models. Design features could include stylish staggered vee-type windscreens, aluminium body panels without joints or mouldings so as to keep the weight down, and plated exhausts, while the interior would be furnished with leather and velour upholstery and fascia trimmings of inlaid polished mahogany.

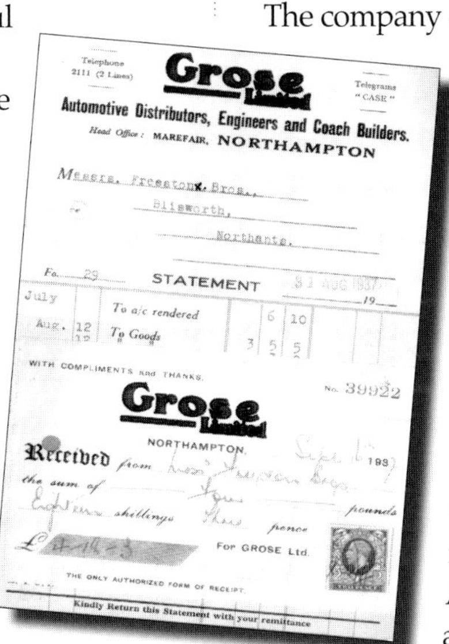

Telephone 2111 (2 Lines)

Grose Limited

Telegrams "CASE"

Automotive Distributors, Engineers and Coach Builders.

Head Office: MAREFAIR, NORTHAMPTON

Messrs. Freestone Bros.,
Blisworth,
Northants.

Fo. 29 STATEMENT 31 AUG 1937 19

July		To a/c rendered	6	10
Aug.	12	To Goods	3 5	5

WITH COMPLIMENTS and THANKS.

No. 39922

Grose Limited

NORTHAMPTON, 193

Received from

the sum of pounds

shillings pence

£

For GROSE Ltd.

THE ONLY AUTHORIZED FORM OF RECEIPT

Kindly Return this Statement with your remittance

However, Grose did not confine its attentions exclusively to the top end of the market. An early economical means of transport was the cyclecar, and one in particular, the Calcott, fitted with Grose's smart two-seater dickey body, sold well locally. After the first world war motorscooters such as the toylike ABC Skootamota, capable of 120 miles per gallon at 20 mph, became popular. From the 1930s, however, the average customer was more likely to purchase a car straight from the production line, so around this time Grose introduced a range of bodies for the various popular chassis, to offer an alternative to the factory options at a lower cost than bespoke coachwork. Known as the village series because the models were named after local villages, this was successful for a while, but as the quality of production-line cars improved, demand for Grose-bodied versions fell.

The company constructed bespoke bodies for all sorts of vehicle chassis, not only private cars. In the commercial market, one of Grose's early creations was a body for trade vehicles which could be taken off and replaced by a touring body for passenger carrying. Although it had been calculated that the cost of running a motor car, at under 3d a mile, was less than half the cost of running a horse, Northampton's tradespeople seem to have been rather slow in making the change, and Grose ran sales drives to promote their vans. As motor transport became established as the norm, commercial vehicle bodywork, mostly purely functional but often with beautifully sign-written panels, became a significant proportion of Grose's work. One of its more unusual commercial bodies, made in 1924 for the Piano Galleries at 32 Abington Street, Northampton, was a low-topped box body, just large enough to hold an upright piano, on a Model T Ford.

Above: *An early invoice issued by the company.*
Top: *A staff outing in the 1920s.*

In 1912 the existing Pike Lane premises were demolished and a new garage was opened, stretching the entire 300 feet length of Pike Lane on the west side. It incorporated a showroom, a suite of offices and a 14,000 square feet garage with a washing bay, three pits and a turntable. Two years later Grose began the Northampton Motor Omnibus Company Limited; from operating one bus which ran between Northampton and Daventry, this developed into an operation with 33 assorted coaches, buses and charabancs and 45 licensed routes including daily services to West Haddon, Welford, Lavendon, Stony Stratford, Weedon and Daventry. However, by 1927 these services had become very time-consuming to run, and the company sold the Northampton Motor Omnibus Company to United Counties.

Grose's bus connection was by no means at an end, however; in 1926 the coachworks had begun work on a fleet of motor coaches for Messrs Du Cros, and the following year Northampton Corporation Tramways Committee ordered four new single-decker buses on Guy B-type chassis. Grose made their first double-decker buses for the borough in 1929. In 1928 Citroen launched a new range of commercial vehicles to complement their existing light vans, and Grose constructed a number of interesting bodies for the lorry chassis; subsequently when Citroen built two new long wheelbase chassis, one for goods and one for passengers, Grose designed a new 20-seater coach for the latter, which became the lowest-priced 20-seater coach on the market and was illustrated in Citroen's catalogue. All the early coaches were metal-on-wood; it was not until the mid 1930s that Grose began to experiment with all-metal coaches.

The company has also constructed hearses, and during both wars many private cars were converted into ambulances; and Grose developed a two-wheeled ambulance trailer to be towed behind a car. Amoured cars and staff cars, often requisitioned from private motorists, were also serviced at Pike Lane.

Mechanisation was introduced early, although some processes were always carried out by hand.

Above: *A 1928 Bean chassis with a Grose van body.*
Top: *The premises in the 1920s.*

The workers worked in teams of four or five, with each gang responsible for the complete construction of a particular body. Only the finest quality leather was used, and the skins were cut in the traditional way, using templates, then stitched into seats and panels.

Woodworkers cut the required pieces out of weathered timber, mostly locally-purchased ash. The joints and bevels were cut, and joiners then assembled the pieces on the chassis, adjusting joints by hand until the fit was perfect and fixing them with screws and angle plates; glue was very rarely used. Aluminium and steel panels, which were attached by brass pins for silence, were roughly shaped by hand with wooden mallets on sandbags, then smoothed on rolling machines, and finally hand planished. The body then went into the paintshop, where in the early days 17 coats of primers, coach-paint and varnish were applied by hand before coachwork cellulose took over, applied by spray; all rubbing down, however, was still done by hand.

The firm celebrated its 50th anniversary by extending the workshops at Pike Lane right through to Horsemarket. The business passed down to the second generation of the family, Kate, Frank and William Thomas, but tragically all three died in a short space of time; fortunately the next generation, William and John, was able to take over. Vehicle sales, rather than carriagework, became the main focus of the company. Shortly after its 75th anniversary the name was changed to Grose Holdings Ltd, the old buildings were sold and new purpose-built five-acre premises at Queen's Park Parade, Kingsthorpe were commissioned, into which they moved in May 1965. The Group continued to expand, mainly through acquisition, and some ten years later Grose Holdings was split into the Northampton branch of W Grose Ltd, controlled by Bill Grose, with Bedford, Vauxhall, Fiat and Volvo agencies, while John established the John Grose Group Ltd, which became a Ford dealership based in Lowestoft.

Times have changed tremendously since the days of Joseph Grose's early ingenious inventions and craftsman-built bespoke carriagework; but in the few examples which survive the company has left classic car enthusiasts with a fine legacy, while the company has successfully changed with the times to continue to serve the motoring public of today.

Thanks to Alan Burman for the use of the photographs on this and the preceding three pages.
His book *Joseph Grose and the Motor Car - a True Pioneer* is published by Phillimore and on sale through all good local bookshops at £14.99.

Above: *A 1920s Grose advertisement.*
Below: *Silverstone in the 1940s with 500cc cars including ones from Grose.*

The College where the standard of education is getting higher and higher

Changes in industrial and economic patterns of an area bring about a corresponding shift in the area's educational needs. This can be clearly seen in Northampton, where over the last century and a half the educational provision has moved forward rapidly to keep pace with the increasingly sophisticated skills required by successive generations. Northampton's Trade School of the late 19th century has risen to the status of University College by the end of the 20th century, and its evolution will continue; the next step will bring full University standing, which will be a true reflection of its achievements in bringing excellence in education to Northampton.

Until the mid-19th century, the people of Northampton gathered all the knowledge they needed from their trade guilds, the apprenticeship system and, of course, the Church; there was no formal educational institute there until the Mechanics' Institute was established in 1833. By this time the industrial revolution was well under way, and the advantages of providing basic education and training, highlighted by the 1870 Education Act, were becoming more widely recognised. Those seeking to further their education in Northampton in 1867 could choose from classes in magnetism and electricity, or drawing and illustration; and the town's very first batch of prizewinning students received their prizes from Earl Spencer at a ceremony in 1868.

1870 saw the establishment of the Trade School in the Mechanics' Institute; soon it moved to the Grammar School in Abington Square, and the curriculum began to expand. Chemistry and agricultural subjects were introduced; the boot and shoe classes which started in 1885 would no doubt have been particularly well-attended; plumbing was added in 1887; but as more and more disciplines were offered, the premises became uncomfortably overcrowded. In 1894 this problem was compounded when art, science and technology were all merged within the existing Grammar School, to form the Northampton and County Modern and Technical School. However, the Art School moved to separate premises in Abington Street in 1907, and four years later the Grammar School relocated to its present site in Billing Road. The Abington Square site now became Northampton Technical School.

Prior to the Great War, teaching and learning had been part-time activities; however, after the end of the war the Technical School employed its first full-time members of staff in the most popular section - boot and shoe manufacture. The School's facilities were extended to include a separate training factory and tannery, and full-time courses in leather-based subjects

Above: *The advert for the 1867 Public Meeting which led to the establishment of the art and science classes, the forerunners of technical education locally.* ***Right:*** *The College in the early days.*

THE STORY OF TECHNICAL EDUCATION IN NORTHAMPTON

When Technical Education Was Taught In A Museum

Early Pioneers' Triumphs Over Difficulties

Royal Opening of The College of Technology

Northampton's Great Lead In Industrial Education

started in 1919, beginning a long tradition of excellence.

The Arts School had, meanwhile, been renamed the School of Arts and Crafts in 1917.

Enrolment on courses at the Technical School increased steadily, and once again the shortage of space began causing problems. By the 1920s the town had acknowledged the need for a permanent institution which would continue to provide education and training in the various disciplines called for by the growing economy, and it began looking for a long-term home for its Technical College. In 1924 a site in St George's Avenue was identified; this site was found suitable and duly purchased for the sum of £7,000, and planning commenced. Construction work began in 1931, and the following year the College was opened by the Duke and Duchess of York. In fact, at the time of the official opening only a part of the planned £80,000 building had been completed, due to financial stringencies. The Technology wing was built first; the east wing, which was to be the Art wing, remained under construction for a further five years, and could not be used until 1937. This did not, however, dampen the enthusiasm with which the local press greeted the opening of the new Northampton Technical College in 1932, and their optimistic claims that University-level education was on its way to Northampton, exaggerated as they might have seemed to some people at the time, were in fact an accurate prediction of future developments.

NORTHAMPTON COUNTY BOROUGH
EDUCATION COMMITTEE

FORMAL OPENING
OF THE
COLLEGE OF TECHNOLOGY
ST. GEORGE'S AVENUE, ON THURSDAY,
NOVEMBER 17TH 1932, AT 11.30 A.M.
BY H.R.H.
THE DUKE OF YORK
H.R.H. WILL BE ACCOMPANIED BY H.R.H. THE
DUCHESS OF YORK

When the second world war was declared, the still-new Northampton Technical College offered an ideal location for military instruction classes and for retraining large numbers of workers for war work. Resuming its normal activities after the war, the College continued to extend its choice of courses, offering National Certificate and City and Guilds courses in a wide range of subjects. In 1956 the government published a White Paper on Technical Education which encouraged institutions to progress towards higher education. Such a move was not, however, appropriate for Northampton College of Technology and Art, as it became known, at this stage; its main emphasis was on practical and vocational education, where it consistently achieved excellent results, and the attainment of high academic standards was not an obvious priority for students whose careers still lay in the traditional local manufacturing trades and industries. To continue to meet the needs of these students, new workshops were added in the next

This page, all pictures: *The opening was a grand affair, reported in the local papers.*

November 26th, 1932. THE NORTHAMPTON AND COUNTY INDEPENDENT 11

An Event Of Importance To World Industry

THE DUKE'S CORDIAL GREETING for Mr. S. S. Campion, J.P., H.F., on arrival at the College. Left to right at rear are Mrs. H. J. Chown, Councillor A. W. Lyne, J.P., and Councillor Sydney Adnitt.

THE PRESENTATION OF NORTHAMPTON SHOES. Left to right are the Duchess and Duke of York, Mr. Ernest Bordoli (Secretary, Northampton Boot Manufacturers' Association), Mr. A. H. Hollister, J.P., C.C. (Vice-President, Boot Manufacturers' Federation), Councillor Sydney Strickland, Mr. W. J. Parker (Chairman of the Boot and Shoe Advisory Committee), Mr. C. G. B. Allinson (President, Northampton Boot Manufacturers' Association), and Councillor James Peach (Chairman of the Borough Education Committee).

THE PRINCIPAL OF THE COLLEGE, Mr. John Blakeman, M.A., M.Sc., presented to the Duke and Duchess. During a tour of the College later Mr. Blakeman was called upon to answer a succession of interested enquiries from Their Royal Highnesses concerning the various processes.

programme of building extensions. The new frontage also formed part of this building programme, and this was opened by Jack Longland, Director of Education for Derbyshire, on January 26 1961, by which time the institution had been renamed Northampton Central College of Technology and Art. The last major structural addition to the College before administrative transformations began was the Sports Hall, built in 1968.

It was by now recognised that the area's traditional boot and shoe industry was in severe decline; concurrently Northampton was designated a town for rapid development and expansion, and this gave an added impetus to the provision of many local facilities and services.

Above: *The College of Technology and Art School before the frontage was added in 1961.*
Below and right: *The College today.*

The repercussions of the changes in the economic and social climate resulted in an increasing amount of unsettlement in the educational sphere. A number of advisory bodies had been formed in the 1960s, composed of influential and powerful local figures, and these now proved to be a great source of strength for Central College at a time when it was finding itself beset by a number of strong external influences, resulting in relationships with some rival institutions becoming rather strained for a while.

More schools were being built to cope with the post-war baby boom, and an increased demand for teacher training emerged during the 1960s. Local teacher training provision already existed, at Leicester University's annexes in Kettering Road, Northampton and nearby at Corby, but this was not considered sufficient and in 1968 a new teacher training college was approved, the last new one of its kind in the country. It then emerged that the Department of Education and Science intended to counterbalance this with the closure of a teacher training college elsewhere. The outcome was that Kirby Fields in Liverpool, identified for closure, was merged with the new Northampton College, which

itself was composed of the two Leicester University annexes plus a new intake of students. In spite of the financial constraints which had again become the order of the day, this College of Education was successfully established and became a constituent college of Leicester University's School of Education.

This was a period of radical change and reform in education. November 10 1972, brought Margaret Thatcher, then Secretary of State for Education and Science, to Northampton to perform the official opening of the new Northampton College of Further Education in Booth Lane. Prior to this, Northampton Central College of Technology and Art had been responsible for meeting both the further and the higher education needs of the area; the co-existence of an institution dedicated to the provision of further education meant that Central College could now devote itself to expanding its range of higher education courses.

As a result of another White Paper which proposed the establishment of multi-disciplinary higher education institutions, it was agreed in 1973 that the new College of Education should be merged with the Colleges of Art and Technology; and out of this came Nene College, opened on October 14 1975 by Lord Crowther-Hunt, Minister of State for Further and Higher Education and enrolling some 2,000 students in that year, with plans to increase this number to 3,200 by 1981. By 1988 student numbers had risen to 4,200 FTE (full-time equivalent). Nene was by now an established and rapidly-developing institution. In 1977, it had merged with the National Leathersellers Centre; in 1982 the Blackwood Hodge Management Centre was opened, followed in 1988 by the Timken Business and Innovation Centre. A merger with Northampton School of Chiropody, now the School of Podiatry, led to a considerable expansion of Nene's healthcare education, and was followed by mergers with the School of Nursing from the General Hospital, and the School of Occupational Therapy at St Andrew's Hospital.

In the late 1980s the government began moves to take many non-university institutions out of local authority control and make them separate corporations, and this plan took effect in 1989. As an independent body, Nene continued to develop. It became a degree-awarding body in 1993; and on January 22 1998 the Government proposed a new category of higher education institution, composed of those colleges of higher education who, like Nene College, have their own degree-awarding powers. As a result, the college has now taken the title of University College Northampton.

Throughout its history, the institution has succeeded admirably in meeting the needs of the people it served. In 1995 the Higher Education Quality Council praised the College's 'high aspirations . . which . . will stand it in good stead'; and thanks to the hard work of all those who have been connected with the institution throughout its many changes, these aspirations are well on their way to becoming achievements.

Top: *The Exhibition Gallery.*
Above left: *Information technology classes.*

150 years of legal history

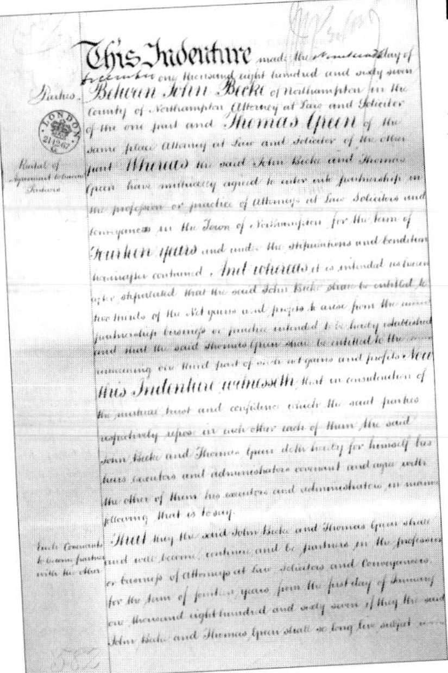

Parties

Recital of Agreement between Partners

Each Covenants to become partner with the other

This Indenture made the nineteenth day of December one thousand eight hundred and sixty seven Between John Becke of Northampton in the County of Northampton Attorney at Law and Solicitor of the one part and Thomas Green of the same place Attorney at Law and Solicitor of the other part Whereas the said John Becke and Thomas Green have mutually agreed to enter into partnership in the profession or practice of Attorneys at Law Solicitors and Conveyancers in the Town of Northampton for the term of fourteen years and under the stipulations and conditions hereinafter contained And whereas it is intended as hereinafter stipulated that the said John Becke shall be entitled to two thirds of the net gains and profits to arise from the said partnership business or practice intended to be hereby established and that the said Thomas Green shall be entitled to the remaining one third part of such net gains and profits Now this Indenture witnesseth that in consideration of the mutual trust and confidence which the said parties respectively repose in each other each of them the said John Becke and Thomas Green doth hereby for himself his heirs executors and administrators covenant and agree with the other of them his executors and administrators in manner following that is to say

That they the said John Becke and Thomas Green shall and will become continue and be partners in the profession or business of Attorneys at Law Solicitors and Conveyancers for the term of fourteen years from the first day of January one thousand eight hundred and sixty seven if they the said John Becke and Thomas Green shall so long live subject

The prestigious legal partnership Hewitson Becke and Shaw has a long and interesting history that can be traced back as far as 1844. When John Becke JP, a gifted lawyer who moved into Northampton from Worcester, founded his practice in the early years of the 19th century, he little knew that the small firm would eventually form part of a wide-ranging regional partnership.

A well-known figure in the community, Mr Becke was appointed Borough Coroner in 1847, and was a founder and Hon Secretary of the Victoria Dispensary. His son Charles Becke, who had obviously inherited his father's acumen and enthusiasm, followed him into the firm and eventually became Coroner and Registrar of the Probate Office. Outside office hours, politics was Charles Becke's great interest and he organised nine elections in Northamptonshire on behalf of Lord Althorp, winning seven out of the nine.

Over the many intervening years the firm has metamorphosed through a number of partnerships and changes of name.

On Mr Becke forming a partnership with Mr T Green in 1867 the firm became known as Becke and Green, and in a key move in 1903 John F Stops, who was articled with Mr Becke not long

Top left: *A page from the original Deed of Partnership, dated 1867.*
Below: *Becke, Green & Stops celebration dinner in 1948 to celebrate the 40th year since Mr Charles Ernest Burton joined the business.*

after he had qualified as a lawyer, was taken into partnership. He worked with the firm of Becke, Green and Stops for an amazing 45 years. He became Under-Sheriff of the county, and as such was responsible for the arrangement of more than 50 Assizes. Mr Stops was not only an eminent solicitor but was at the same time well known in sporting circles as a genuine all-round sportsman. Athletics, cricket, Association football, rugby, hockey, tennis, golf - all were grist to this amazing man's mill. He played for the county in most of his sports, played soccer for Northampton Banks, became a rugby forward for the Saints and became president of the Saints' Club in 1930. Later he played centre forward at hockey for Northampton and for the county and was made captain of the Brampton Golf Club, representing the county in the game.

A veteran of World War I, during which he was a captain with the Coldstream Guards, the years of the second world war saw Mr Stops working with the various wartime charities as secretary of Northamptonshire Red Cross and St John and Kindred Associations. After his death in 1944 the business was carried on by Mr Charles E Burton, who had been articled to Mr Green in 1908, and Mr T Faulkner Gammage, who had joined the firm in 1937. Mr Gammage became Northampton Borough Coroner in 1952, earning a reputation as being singularly humane and understanding in that position. For 24 years he also acted as clerk at the Northampton Divisional and Daventry Divisional Courts, and as clerk to the Commissioners for both the Northampton and Daventry Divisions. He had been both president and treasurer of Northamptonshire Law Society. Outside business hours Mr Gammage proved to be another active sportsman, keen on rock climbing and golf. Twice he captained Northamptonshire County Golf Club and was president of the county's Golf Union.

After the Second World War Charles Mumby, a solicitor with a wide professional interest, joined Mr Burton and Mr Gammage in the partnership.

Mr Gammage retired as senior partner in the law practice in 1968 - though he remained in the wings as a consultant. After his retirement the practice underwent further changes at the end of the year when Becke, Green & Stops amalgamated with distinguished local lawyers Phipps & Troup, with whom they had long held personal ties and friendships. The strengths of the two were complementary to each other, and the partnership carried on the joint practices under the name of Becke, Phipps & Co, continuing in their premises at Spencer Parade and at Market Square. In February 1969 the firm amalgamated with another law practice, Hensman Jackson & Chamberlain, retaining the name Becke, Phipps & Co.

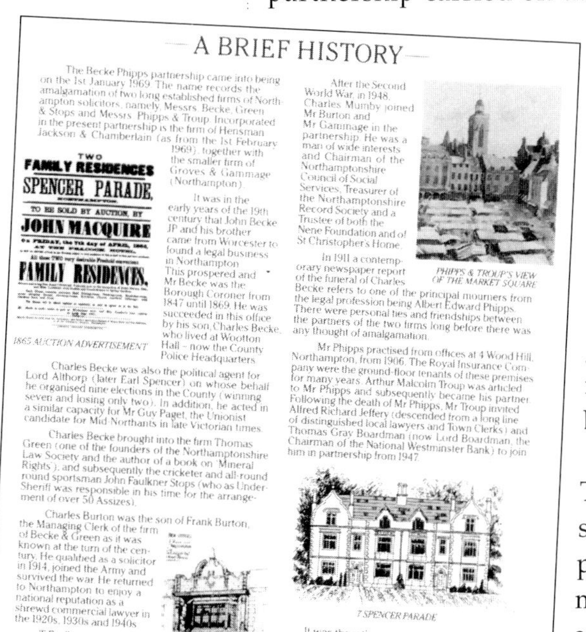

A BRIEF HISTORY

The Becke Phipps partnership came into being on the 1st January 1969. The name records the amalgamation of two long established firms of Northampton solicitors, namely, Messrs. Becke, Green & Stops and Messrs. Phipps & Troup. Incorporated in the present partnership is the firm of Hensman Jackson & Chamberlain (as from the 1st February 1969), together with the smaller firm of Groves & Gammage (Northampton).

1865 AUCTION ADVERTISEMENT

It was in the early years of the 19th century that John Becke JP and his brother came from Worcester to found a legal business in Northampton. This prospered and Mr Becke was the Borough Coroner from 1847 until 1869. He was succeeded in this office by his son, Charles Becke, who lived at Wootton Hall – now the County Police Headquarters.

Charles Becke was also the political agent for Lord Althorp (later Earl Spencer) on whose behalf he organised nine elections in the County (winning seven and losing only two). In addition, he acted in a similar capacity for Mr Guy Paget, the Unionist candidate for Mid Northants in late Victorian times.

Charles Becke brought into the firm Thomas Green (one of the founders of the Northamptonshire Law Society and the author of a book on 'Mineral Rights'), and subsequently the cricketer and all-round sportsman John Faulkner Stops (who as Under-Sheriff was responsible in his time for the arrangement of over 50 Assizes).

Charles Burton was the son of Frank Burton, the Managing Clerk of the firm of Becke & Green as it was known at the turn of the century. He qualified as a solicitor in 1914, joined the Army and survived the war. He returned to Northampton to enjoy a national reputation as a shrewd commercial lawyer in the 1920s, 1930s and 1940s.

T Faulkner Gammage became a partner in Becke Green & Stops towards the end of the 1930s on the death of his own partner, Mr W Yorke Groves, and is remembered as a fine advocate and as the last part-time Clerk to the County Justices, as well as being a notable County and Borough Coroner.

4 WOOD HILL

After the Second World War, in 1948, Charles Mumby joined Mr Burton and Mr Gammage in the partnership. He was a man of wide interests and Chairman of the Northamptonshire Council of Social Services, Treasurer of the Northamptonshire Record Society and a Trustee of both the Nene Foundation and of St Christopher's Home.

PHIPPS & TROUP'S VIEW OF THE MARKET SQUARE

In 1911 a contemporary newspaper report of the funeral of Charles Becke refers to one of the principal mourners from the legal profession being Albert Edward Phipps. There were personal ties and friendships between the partners of the two firms long before there was any thought of amalgamation.

Mr Phipps practised from offices at 4 Wood Hill, Northampton, from 1906. The Royal Insurance Company were the ground-floor tenants of these premises for many years. Arthur Malcolm Troup was articled to Mr Phipps and subsequently became his partner. Following the death of Mr Phipps, Mr Troup invited Alfred Richard Jeffery (descended from a long line of distinguished local lawyers and Town Clerks) and Thomas Gray Boardman (now Lord Boardman, the Chairman of the National Westminster Bank) to join him in partnership from 1947.

7 SPENCER PARADE

It was the retirement of Mr Gammage and the election to Parliament of Mr Boardman that brought the partnerships together in 1969, since it was appreciated that the strengths of the two were complementary.

This brief review illustrates how Becke Phipps in its various component parts, has practised locally for almost 200 years. Over this period its partners have been involved in the private and public affairs of the Town and County. Their contributions to the life of Northampton have been both collective and individual. It is this tradition which the present partners seek to continue.

The wide-ranging services offered by the partnership covered the many branches of the law and included company formations, conveyancing, partnership, probate, debt collection and many more, their team of experienced solicitors and legal executives covering personal needs as well as the needs of companies. Taking advantage of modern technology as it became available, the go-ahead practice seized the

***Above:** A page of their history from the first firm brochure.*
***Top right**: Death certificate of Mr Charles R Becke, dated 1911.*

opportunity of commissioning specifically-designed software programmes such as that used by the Debt Collection Department, which enabled between 4,000 and 5,000 tasks to be handled at any one time. In charge of the latest technology was senior partner Alfred Jeffery who, at an amazing 80 years old, was a computer 'whizz-kid'.

The year 1984 saw a relaxation of restrictions - within limits - on advertising the services of professional bodies. Becke Phipps were among the first to publish a colour brochure advertising their services, from negligence and personal injury to bankruptcy and liquidation, from purchases and sales to separation and divorce. In charge of personal injury claims, medical negligence, family law and child care cases was Anne Rees, who in 1985 became Becke Phipps' first female partner.

A further exciting merger took place in 1989, when Becke Phipps amalgamated with the respected Cambridge legal practice Wild Hewitson and Shaw. The two practices had long shared the same philosophy of a commerical outlook and recruitment of high quality staff and the high level of personal service they offered to their clients, and the result of the merger was Hewitson Becke and Shaw - one of the top ten legal firms outside London.

The enlarged practice, with 40 partners, one consultant and a staff of 280, covered extensive areas of the East Midlands and East Anglia, and had a network of offices in Northampton, Cambridge, Saffron Walden, Bishop's Stortford and Newmarket. Another office was opened in Peterborough by the end of the year. The merger offered clients the benefit of a wide local knowledge accumulated by the team over many years of experience, and the added number of solicitors were able to cover the increasing areas of specialisation in depth.

Above: *Charles Ernest Burton's probate from 1954.*
Below: *The company premises at 6 & 7 Spencer Parade.*

The period of tremendous growth that followed the merger demanded more up to date technology, and in 1990 a new £250,000 fully networked computer system was installed, enabling all the offices to communicate with each other by computer. The new system ensured the fast and secure transfer of data between the offices, providing a more comprehensive and speedier service to clients.

The following year saw the appointment of Keith Davidson, who was head of the practice's Corporate Department for the East Midlands, as Hewitson Becke & Shaw's new Senior Partner. He took over from Peter Shaw, who had steered the firm through its recent successful merger and expansion, though Mr Shaw continued as an active partner in the firm, working a four-day week. In 1994 Ian Barnett took over the role of Senior Partner when in turn Keith Davidson decided to reduce his own working week.

During their long and distinguished history the various partners in Hewitson Becke & Shaw have played a key role, both privately and publicly, in the affairs of Northampton - and across the East Midlands and East Anglia. The practice has continued to go from strength to strength - and the partnership that has risen to so many challenges in the past is well equipped to go forward to face the exciting challenges that lie ahead.

BECKE PHIPPS

BUSINESS NEWSLETTER

Autumn Issue

A FRESH TALENT IN COMMERCIAL LAW

Richard Ingram (no connection with the former Editor of Private Eye) joined the Company Department at Becke Phipps at the beginning of June.

Richard and his wife Kay both come from Kettering. Richard was educated at Wellingborough School, and spent a year at the Kettering office of accountants Grant Thornton before reading law at Downing College, Cambridge.

After Cambridge, he went on to law school at Guildford where he was a Law Society prize-winner in the professional examinations. He then spent five years as a company and commercial lawyer at Allen & Overy, a leading firm of London solicitors. This was followed by a further three years at a major Bristol practice where he broadened his experience of the sort of corporate and business issues that arise outside London. His main interest in law now lies in merger and acquisition work, and in advising clients on corporate finance matters.

He and his wife have settled in Weston Favell with their three children.

Out of office hours, Richard is interested in a number of sports and when he has the time, he particularly likes to play golf.

In this Issue . . . .

Trading Terms — a vital consideration for your business 2
Acquisition of Companies — The Hidden Risks 4
The Revenue back down on the Taxation of 'Earn Outs' 5

Left: *An internal business newsletter from 1988.* ***Below:*** *The current Senior Partner, Ian Barnett (back row, second left) with past High Sheriffs of Northamptonshire, celebrating his 25 years as Under-Sheriff in 1998.*

The story of the 'Dick Whittington' of Northampton

Oliver Adams is a familiar name in Northamptonshire. The bakery is well-known for supplying high quality bread and confectionery in its nineteen shops throughout the county, and beyond. The firm started in 1856, in a small back street near Lady's Lane.

The man who started the business was Thomas Adams - a more Dick Whittington-like figure it would be hard to imagine. In 1847, from a humble family home in Flore, Thomas walked to Northampton with all his worldly goods over his shoulder, by chance became apprenticed to a baker, after nine years had become a Master Baker, and by the age of 55 had twice been elected Mayor of Northampton.

Thomas had nine children, four of whom continued the bakery business and ensured its steady expansion throughout the town. Thomas was thus able to follow his political leanings, becoming a councillor and also a keen supporter of the famous Radical M.P., Charles Bradlaugh.

Not only was Thomas active politically, eventually becoming Mayor of Northampton; he was also involved in the early building society movement, the prime motive for which was to enable the working class man to own a house and thereby have the right to vote. In fact several of his sons carried on his work by becoming directors of the building society which is now the Nationwide.

The firm's most momentous occasion in the 20th century was the opening of a brand new bakery at Kings Heath in 1951 when the family amalgamated their separate businesses and became the largest independent bakery in town.

To celebrate the firm's achievement in spanning three centuries as a leading Northampton bakery, a book by Jane Evans is to be published for the millennium which will bring together the fascinating stories of the enterprising family behind the name 'Oliver Adams'.

Above: *The West Street shop at the turn of the century.*
Top left: *Thomas Adams and Elizabeth Oliver, who married in March 1857.*
Below: *The Wood Hill premises in the 1960s.*

(Probably) Northampton's most famous company

The Carlsberg-Tetley Brewery at Northampton stands on the site of the former Northampton Brewery Company, which began brewing in 1846. Older readers will still remember some of the Northampton Brewery pubs, which in 1956, when the brewery celebrated its centenary, included the Boothville which subsequently became the Lumbertub, the Clicker, the Sunnyside, the Westone and the Red Earl, subsequently renamed the Dallington Brook. During the 50s, however, the small brewers had to struggle to contend with competition from bottled beers; the Northampton Brewing Company was unable to finance construction of a bottling plant, and later that year the NBC began discussions with Phipps which resulted in a merger between the two companies.

Above: *An early Tetley Showcard.*
Below: *A pumping engine c1866.*

The range of beers produced at this time included Ratcliffe and Jumbo stout, Buffalo Brown, Phipps PA and Starlight, and the successful Stein, which was first brewed in May 1959 and won a silver medal at the British Bottlers Institute exhibition in the Isle of Man. However, the economic climate was making it increasingly difficult for small independent breweries to survive; PNBC became part of the Watney Mann Group, Phipps' old claret-coloured signboards and the NBC houses' black facades were replaced by the red Watney corporate image and Watney's Red Barrel took over as the Group's main product. In 1968 the name of the company was changed to Watney Mann (Midlands) and the brewing of traditional ales ceased. The site eventually became home to a new Carlsberg Brewery designed by Copenhagen architect, Knud Munk, which was

inaugurated by HRH Princess Benedikte on 10th May 1974. In August 1975 further praise was given when the new brewery won the Financial Times Industrial Architectural award. The Carlsberg plant was a showcase for modern brewing methods and innovative industrial technology; but there will always be some very important processes which man would be foolish to delegate to machine. So every day 'blind' taste test panels sit and sample lagers, assessing them for quality.

The data from these samplings is sent back for analysis to Copenhagen, where Captain J C Jacobsen launched Denmark's first lager beer in 1847 - almost the same time that the Northampton Brewery Company began. The site he chose was a small town set on a hill overlooking Copenhagen, and the literal translation of 'Carlsberg' is 'Carl's hill'; Carl was the name of Captain Jacobsen's son.

Carlsberg lager was brought to Britain by the Danish sea captains of the mid-19th century, who kindly shared their personal drinking supplies with friends in British ports. Britain was quick to acquire the taste; Edinburgh's port of Leith was importing regular stocks from 1868, and by the mid 1900s the phenomenal success of Carlsberg lager throughout the UK had resulted in the founding of three separate trading companies, with some 50 brewers and bottling companies becoming distributors for the brand.

In 1950 Carlsberg Special Brew was introduced to commemorate the visit of Winston Churchill to Copenhagen. This dark, very strong lager was immediately liked by discerning drinkers, and it has remained a market leader ever since. At 9.0% ABV it is Carlsberg's strongest lager; the other Carlsberg brands are draught or bottled Carlsberg Lager at 3.8% ABV; canned Carlsberg Lager at 4.2% ABV; draught, canned or bottled Carlsberg Export at 5.0% ABV; bottled Carlsberg Ice Beer at 5.0%; and bottled Carlsberg Elephant Beer at 7.2% ABV. Elephant Beer, which derived its name from the imposing Elephant Gate entrance to the Carlsberg Breweries in Copenhagen, was launched in the UK in 1989 and is highly rated by connoisseurs of imported lagers. Ice Beer is Carlsberg's newest product; launched in 1994, it is brewed with the unique 'Ice Brewing' process which results in a beer with a crisp, mellow taste with extraordinary balance. All Carlsberg lagers are brewed using the Danish yeast Saccharomyces Casbergensis, Carlsberg's very own yeast, which has in fact become the derivative for all modern-day lager yeasts; and a detailed set of guidelines is issued to every on-trade stockist, to ensure that the lager is handled and stored correctly and served to the consumer in peak condition.

The UK is Carlsberg's oldest and largest international market, with a million pints of Carlsberg Lager sold here every day - on average, 23 pints every second. The premium lager market is currently enjoying the most marked expansion, with consumer preference shifting towards premium lagers of 4.3% ABV to 7.4% ABV; off-licence sales of Carlsberg Special Brew, the UK's best-selling superstrength lager, run at 150 cans a minute. Worldwide, Carlsberg exports to over 130 countries, and is the second largest brewer in the world.

In 1992 Carlsberg UK merged with Allied Breweries, the brewing division of Allied Lyons, now Allied Domecq. Originally a joint venture, with Carlsberg and Allied Domecq each owning 50% stake, Carlsberg-Tetley became 100% owned by Carlsberg A/S in January 1998. Employing over 2,500 people in the UK, the company has an extensive product portfolio which includes Tetley's Bitter and Calder's Premium Cream Beer along with brands such as Castlemaine XXXX which are brewed under licence, as well as the Carlsberg range.

Customer research shows that the UK's younger lager drinkers are the thirstiest, with the 18-24 age group consuming the most beer, and Carlsberg's generous sponsorship of sports and music events has won it immense popularity with young people. A sponsor of the European Football Championships since 1982 and Liverpool Football Club since 1992, Carlsberg was also the Official Beer of the FA Cup, the European Cup Winners Cup and the UEFA Cup, and is imprinted forever on the memory of millions of football-lovers as Official Beer of the England Team in the World Cup '98 - the second biggest sporting event ever staged. In Rugby Union, Tetley's Bitter is now the Official Beer of England Rugby and is the title sponsor of the Tetley's Bitter Cup as well as giving further support to the county championship, the Under-21 county championship and the RFU Junior Cup which is now called the Tetley's Bitter Vase. On the music scene, Carlsberg currently sponsors the MTV Music Awards, and has quenched the thirst of festival-goers at the Glastonbury, Phoenix and Reading Music Festivals since 1990; and one of the musical highlights of 1997 was the Carlsberg Concert '97, held at Wembley Stadium to celebrate the company's 150th birthday. Featuring stars such as Jon Bon Jovi, Rod Stewart and Seal, the concert attracted an audience of 84,000 and was screened on BBC-1 and worldwide to a further half a billion viewers.

Although Carlsberg is a household name, the company has never become complacent and continues to monitor the marketplace to ensure that its products never lose their appeal. When, for instance, the name Pilsner began to be adopted by cheaper, lower strength brands in the early 1990s, Carlsberg immediately responded by changing the name of its Carlsberg Pilsner to Carlsberg Lager, and relaunching the product with new packaging, an increased alcohol by volume content, and improved taste, texture and body.

Carlsberg's 'Probably the best lager in the world' advertising campaign has become legendary, running as it has for 25 years which makes it one of the longest-running campaigns for any product, and amongst the famous personalities who have appeared in its 100-plus commercials are Orson Welles, James Coburn and Ian Botham.

Part of the secret of Carlsberg-Tetley's success, it seems, is its commitment to pleasing its public. Whether it be in its advertising, in the sporting and musical events which it promotes, or in brewing (probably) the best draught and take-home lager in the world, Carlsberg-Tetley excels in giving its customers exactly what they want.

***Facing page:** The Carlsberg-Tetley Brewery in Northampton.*
***Left:** Carlsberg-Tetley sponsors many events such as rugby as seen here.*

"A College which exists to serve the community"

That was the description used by Lord Belstead, the then Parliamentary Under-Secretary of State for Education and Science, when he performed the official opening ceremony of Northampton College on Friday 18 May 1973.

Since then the College has seen many changes but its mission is still very much focused on the needs of Northampton and its immediate locality.

Toward the end of the 1960s the Borough Council Education Committee and the Chief Education officer at the time, MJ Henley MA, identified the need for a new college of further education in Northampton to complement the existing College of Technology and School of Art. The need arose from continuing pressure on the accommodation available at those establishments and the anticipated expansion of the population over the period 1971 to 1981.

The first phase of the building project was included by the Department of Education and Science in the 1968-69 preliminary list and building began in November 1970. The first stage of the initial building programme was completed in time to welcome new students in September 1972. Phase Two of the buildings were completed in time for the September 1974 in-take. Since then, increasing work and the expanding student population has meant that new building works have been a common occurrence on campus.

In addition to its main campus at Booth Lane, which houses the majority of the College's work including all full-time courses, the College runs a wide range of educational, leisure and recreational courses at many centres throughout Northampton, through its Community Programme sponsored by Northamptonshire County Council Education and Community Learning Adult Education Services.

The Chairman of Northampton County Borough Education Committee, who welcomed Lord Belstead to the official opening ceremony, was reported as saying at the time: "...the age range

Below: *The College as it appeared in the early 1970s.*

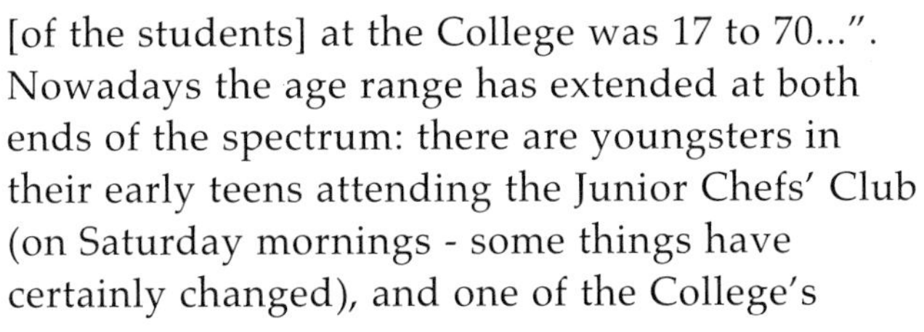

[of the students] at the College was 17 to 70...". Nowadays the age range has extended at both ends of the spectrum: there are youngsters in their early teens attending the Junior Chefs' Club (on Saturday mornings - some things have certainly changed), and one of the College's recent National Adult Learners' Award Week Nominees was an active and enthusiastic centenarian. 'Education for Life' is something the College takes very seriously and it is committed to supporting the campaign for Life-long Learning.

Northampton College is very much aware of its importance in the life of the local community and the role it has in the local economy - both in terms of being a major employer and a provider of education and training. It is pleased to work in partnership with many of the area's employers and the Northamptonshire Chamber and others involved in education and training, in seeking to enhance the employment prospects of the region's workforce, and the continuing prosperity of its population.

Northampton College is proud of its achievements and the significant contribution it has made over the last quarter century, and looks forward with eagerness and anticipation to the opportunities and challenges that the new millennium will bring.

Above left: *The College Annual Awards Ceremony Presentation held at the Guildhall, Northampton.*
Above right: *The Northampton College production of 'The Stand' at the Edinburgh Festival in 1998.*
Left: *The College today.*

Everybody would like to be in this family's shoes . . .

King Alfred may not have been very reliable when it came to baking cakes, but he could be depended on to recognise a good boot when he saw one. We know this from history, which records that he had boots for his troops made in Northampton, later acknowledged as the home of high-quality shoemaking; and if Church's had been in business around the year 900, King Alfred would surely have patronised them.

In fact, Church's factory was set up in 1873 by Alfred and William Church, with their father, Thomas. The family had a long tradition of shoemaking; Stone Church, the great-great grand-father of the founders, was making shoes as far back as 1675, and the craft had been passed down from father to son.

Before very long the family firm moved from its small workshop in Maple Street to a factory in Duke Street. The firm clearly prospered as the 1885 Northampton Directory lists the brothers as Resident Gentry. As business grew, William took responsibility for selling, and Alfred was in charge of manufacturing. Church's manufactured a wide range of quality shoes, with names such as Walkinease, Marcheasy, Antifag, and boot called Adapted which won a Gold Medal at the Great Exhibition at Crystal Palace. William was quick to exploit the export market; he employed a salesman to work in Europe and began to export to France in 1904. Special 'lasts' were made for the US market and shoes were sold on the West Coast and in Canada. The emphasis remained on quality; in 1913, when cheap shoes could be bought for half a crown, Church's Footform men's shoes were priced at 16s 9d and boots at £1 2s 6d, with women's shoes at 14s 9d and boots at 18s 6d. And it was Church's who made the shoes which were presented to the little Royal Princess when King George and Queen Mary visited Northampton in 1913.

Above: *Thomas Church, founder of the company and father of the other founders.*
Below: *Babers - the interior of the old shop.*

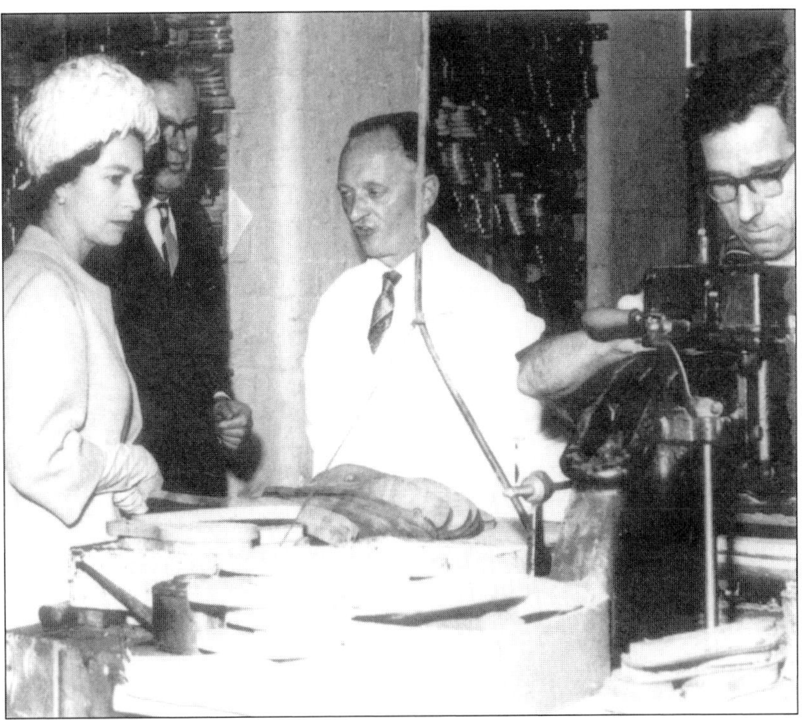

Alfred's son Leslie joined the partnership in 1913, but was almost immediately called up, as were his cousins Basil and Dudley. A tremendous number of army boots were required during the war years, and all Northampton's shoe manufacturers were kept busy. The year between the wars saw increased production of women's shoes, which had previously not been a significant line, and the concept of fashion rather than utiliarianism began to play a role in shoe design; however, the second world war more footwear for the armed forces, and it was not until the mid 50s that the shoe industry was really able to turn its attention to the new generation of affluent, fashion-conscious young consumers. Church's shoes around this time included the famous Coach-hide brogue and Archmoulded shoes such as Laredo and Montrose. By now a number of high class independent retailers, including Oxford Street stores, were stocking the company's goods, and an increasing presence was being established in Scotland, while sales to America continued; and in 1956 Church's itself became a retailer, setting up its own chain of shops.

Throughout the late 50s and 60s the company continued to expand, opening new retail outlets and increasing its exports; computers were introduced; the company moved to the factory at St James which is today its Northampton Headquarters; and Desborough-based firm Cheaneys, who were important suppliers to American and Canadian companies, became part of the Group. New lines such as Fetherflex, Glovemocs, Slipmocs and Scintillas, introduced in response to the demand for lighter weight casuals, proved very popular, and the Company celebrated its centenary in 1973 as an expanding concern going from strength to strength. By the end of the 70s, Church's export customers included Sweden, France and Belgium, and the 80s saw further expansion, including joint ownership of a new company retailing in Hong Kong. Trade in the Far Eastern grew with the formation of Church Japan in 1992, and this trend is set to continue.

In its rise to international recognition, the Group has been led by an unbroken line of descendants from the brothers who founded the firm more than 125 years ago. Many of these have been eminent industrialists in their own right; John Church, the current Chairman, is grandson of the founder and an active international Trade Leader. Over the years, many new ideas and a surprising amount of mechanisation have been adopted, but only where this retains or raises quality standards, and an enormous amount of hand-care is still employed in the handling and making of Church's shoes. The company has done much to build the reputation for quality which British shoes enjoy worldwide, and this is due the commitment and dedication of successive generations of the Church family - makers of quality footwear for more than three centuries.

Above: *Dale Street canteen in the 1950s.*
Top: *The Queen's visit in 1965.*
Left: *John Church (son of Dudley Church), Group Chairman and joint Managing Director.*

Business is moving

Wardle and Keach was formed in 1926 by the amalgamation of two family firms, one of which had been first established in 1890 and the other slightly later. The histories of the original businesses both reflect the continuing development of Northampton during the twentieth century.

Albert Wardle came from the village of Kegworth to manage Liptons in Kettering. At the age of forty he went into partnership in 1900 with Mr Jacques who died a few years later. Messrs A Wardle and Son, founded in 1905, continued the coal haulage business, and Harold Wardle took over from his father and ran the business independently into the 1920s.

Meanwhile George Keach from Melton Ernest in Bedfordshire had also migrated to Kettering to make his fortune in the same field. He too delivered coal from horse-drawn vehicles before progressing to general haulage in 1912 when he purchased some steam traction engines. In time the business passed to his son Charles who ran it as a sole trader concern into the 1920s.

The two companies worked side by side, more often in cooperation than in competition, until the young men decided in 1926 that they would benefit by amalgamating. The new partnership of Wardle and Keach operated from the Keach premises in Crown Street where they worked hard to expand the coal business and to develop a furniture enterprise up until the outbreak of war in 1939.

In the war years some of their vital lorries were commandeered for war use and Harold Wardle's son Norman was conscripted into the RAF. Suffering under the strains of running a business under wartime conditions, in 1945 the parents applied to the Air Ministry for the early release of young Norman, but he was not demobilised until the following year.

On his return he found things rather run-down, and the patched-up vehicles running on cannibalised parts, like so many around the country, were literally on their last wheels.

In 1947 Charles Keach's nephew Mr Panter joined Norman Wardle in rebuilding the war-weary company. Their priority was to obtain new lorries, firstly furniture vans to take war evacuees back to their homes in bomb-battered London, then coal lorries; Wardle and Keach supplied 90% of all Kettering factories, plus all the schools in Kettering, Corby and all the surrounding village with their coal rations. The firm collected coal

Above: *Stamford Road, Kettering.*

Below: *Keach's removal van at Woolleston.*

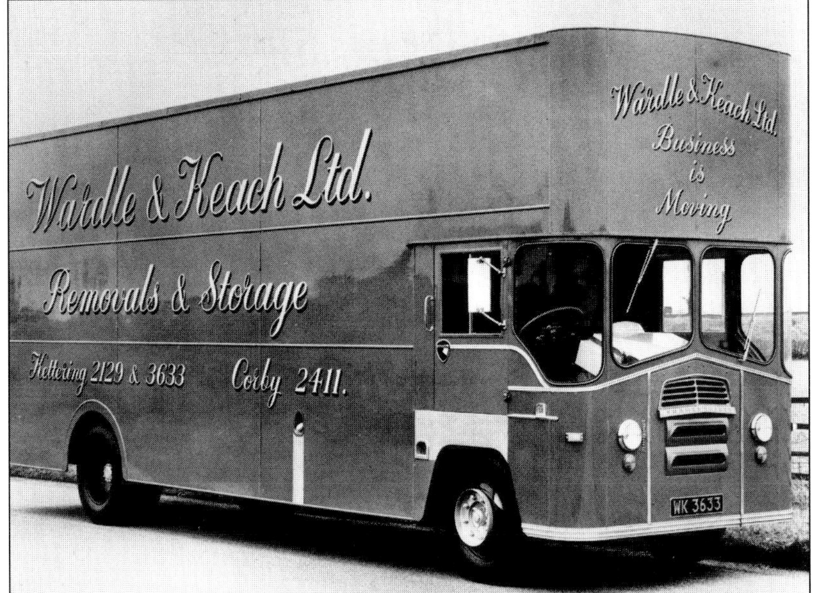

larger site was soon required, and in 1988 they moved to purpose-built warehouse premises on the Brixworth Industrial Estate. The company's current site at Little Houghton was purchased in 1991, and construction of the new warehouse there was completed in 1993. Wardle and Keach's growth has continued through acquisition; Frosts Removals was purchased in 1987, William Olivers in 1991, and more recently Hillyards has become part of the firm. A fleet of eighteen vehicles with expert crews carries out local, national and international removals, and another new warehouse is currently under construction, which when finished will provide 10,000 square feet of containerised storage enabling containers to be stacked four high, while the existing warehouse will be used archive storage, extending the firm's commercial and office removals service to include archiving, complete with a retrieval service.

Paul and Sue Henry's daughter Hannah is now a valued member of the firm. Having performed various tasks such as packing duties and acting as office junior, she went on to obtain a BA Honours degree in Business Studies from Nene College, now University College Northampton, and has recently been promoted to Corporate Accounts and Liaison Officer.

In becoming the largest independent removal company in the area, Wardle and Keach has remained a family-run concern with a caring attitude and a commitment to quality - values which have helped bring about success during this century, and which will without a doubt bring even greater success in the next Millennium.

Top: *An early Thames Trader van.*
Above left: *A near disaster above the M4. The motorway was closed to clear the stricken van away.*
Below: *The company was commissioned to move restored pictures from Althorp in the late 1980s.*

from the nearby collieries in hoppers, setting up a coal depot on plot of land in the town which it had bought for the purpose.

The furniture side of the business was also expanding, and needed storage space, so an empty factory was bought and converted for use as a furniture repository, with lifts installed. The influx of American service families joining airmen stationed at USAF bases at Grafton Underwood, Molesworth and Mildenhall meant that up to ten six to twelve ton loads of crated furniture and possessions were arriving daily, and a fork lift truck was purchased to load and unload the crates. The firm also entered the export business on behalf of the USAF.

Norman Wardle retired in 1985 and his son Peter ran the company briefly but then decided to sell to the proprietors of another local haulage firm, Henry's Removals, who were looking to expand. Paul and Sue Henry became the new owners of Wardle and Keach in 1986, keeping Peter on as company accountant and transferring the business to the premises in Kingswell Street from which Henry's Removals had operated. Under their management expansion was so rapid that a

Clear vision for the future in eyecare and eyewear

Albert Edward Turville's interest in spectacles and eye problems began towards the end of the 19th century when, as a small boy, he would help his father, a Northampton watchmaker and jeweller. Pairs of spectacles were often handed in to the shop for repair, which encouraged the young Albert Edward to take an interest. He had eye problems of his own, and the myopic astigmatism he suffered from fostered his interest in ophthalmic optics. He went on to pass the BOA examination in 1914 and the following year saw him set up a practice in premises that had once housed a doctor's surgery in Abington Street, Northampton. He made his home on the premises, and the consulting room during the day was his sitting room outside working hours.

It was from there that the enthusiastic young ophthalmic optician began to carry out his many research projects. His special interest was in the practical area of instrument design and construction, and over the next 45 years he was to develop many outstanding clinical systems and innovative optical instruments including, in 1927, the prototype for the Turville Stewart ophthalmoscope, hand slit lamp and retinoscope. Turville's publications were many and varied, from papers on his research into sight testing techniques and binocular vision correction to treatments for the partially sighted and migraine sufferers. A leading figure in the British optical world, Mr Turville became advisor to the government during the establishment of the NHS.

His expertise and comprehensive knowledge of his subject gathered over many years combined to earn him a worldwide reputation in the field. In recognition of his activities he was awarded an OBE and he received a number of honorary fellowships for his work internationally. Outside the workplace, Mr Turville had many interests. He was an amateur radio ham in the years before the second world war, which led to an involvement with the Foreign Service Broadcasting - and to espionage during the war!

A key decision was taken in 1964 when John Sheinman joined Mr Turville in the practice. Sadly, A E Turville died only a year later and John was left to carry on alone. Building on his predecessor's reputation, John Sheinman proceeded to develop this remarkable practice into one of the foremost centres for eye care in Europe. 1982-1995 saw a period of intense expansion into the adjoining buildings on either side. Today the practice covers an amazing 10,000 square feet. It is considered to be the largest optometric practice in Europe and the research and development of clinical equipment remains an important part of their work. The vast majority of Sheinman patients come from Northamptonshire, with around five percent living outside the county. The patient's first impression on entering the building is of an extensive and well designed operation. The theme of

Above centre: *Albert Edward Turville, the founder of the Practice.*
Below right: *John Sheinman.*
Below: *A E Turville's 1930s consulting room makes an interesting comparison to the state-of-the-art facilities as found in the Practice today.*

dispensing and the sight testing areas are developed quite separately as in the past, but very naturally blend into a single interdependent unit.

The environment differs from that of most high street practices due to the spacious and relaxed atmosphere. Research rooms on the premises provide the necessary space for ongoing study and investigation, while the firm's optical laboratory was significantly enlarged in recent years to embrace every modern concept of spectacle design and manufacture.

Sheinman Associates provide an exciting and comprehensive choice of frames in a vast showroom, benefiting from natural daylight from an atrium roof. Much admired are the unique viewing stations which allow patients to try on frames while watching themselves on video - an innovative and popular method of choosing a pair of spectacles. In addition, computer programmes show patients how current lens technology relates to their own particular needs, providing a price guide as a useful reference.

And the future....

Sheinman Associates' programme of continued expansion and research will continue to closely involve children's eyecare - an area of study that interestingly had been of particular significance to A E Turville back in the late 1920s. Projects as diverse as computerised sight testing systems, exclusive eyewear design and preserving the sight of the ageing eye also remain at the hub of their activities.

Since Mr Turville set up the practice in 1915, genuine patient care and the ability to offer a more fully comprehensive eyecare service than average has been at the cutting edge of the practice's success. Their aim is to continually explore new and even better ways to provide the most advanced total eyecare service into the next millennium.

Above right: *The entrance reception.* ***Top:*** *The front of the Practice until 1975 - the last 'house' in Abington Street.* ***Right:*** *Today's view of the Practice on Abington Street.*

A sure sign of success

From a one-man electrical installations business established fifty years ago, Hawes Signs has expanded and developed over the years until today the company has contracts with such prestigious companies as Tesco, Asda and Safeway Stores, Nissan Europe NV, British Airways, Texaco, Lloyds TSB, and has a turnover of £20 million.

It was 1949 when Kenneth Hawes set up in business, taking on electrical contracts, carrying out repairs to electric signs, and performing domestic and industrial electrical installations around Islington. Eventually his three sons - who all possessed a great deal of business acumen as well as expertise in engineering technology - joined him in the rapidly expanding firm. Their backgrounds in engineering and the sign industry were crucial to the business, as they brought with them an unparalleled combination of knowledge and experience. Keith Hawes was appointed as Managing Director, Clive Hawes became Business Development Director and Nigel Hawes was made Field Services Director.

In a move to the Northampton area, Hawes Signs took over Brilite Signs, who had premises in Earl Street. The 1950s and 60s were years of steady growth; it was in the 1960s that the company formed their first links with Tesco, a continuing customer to the present day. In 1973 further expansion took the firm to Gray Street, and in 1982 they moved to the site of the present premises in Moulton Park. At the time the move gave them 12,500 square feet of office space and 40,000 square feet of manufacturing and storage space. In 1988 a large plot of adjacent land was acquired, giving Hawes Signs a seven-acre site. An additional factory and warehouse were built, making a total of 15,000 square feet devoted to offices, and 65,000 square feet given over to manufacturing and storage.

Hawes Signs was by now an extremely successful company, with contracts both in the UK and overseas. They generated a comprehensive Pan-European activity with companies such as Nissan and Fina. Instrumental to the company's success was their understanding of the strict time schedules that the contracts demanded, and the importance of delivering products and services to clients within an agreed budget while at the same time maintaining quality standards and integrity of design. The company eventually became a 25% equity partner of ECCE Signs for Europe BV, an

Above: *The staff in the welding room in the 1970s.*
Left: *The installation fleet in the 1950s.*

Amsterdam-based joint venture company that provides overseas clients with a comprehensive Pan-European service.

Investment into the latest technology through the years has kept Hawes Signs at the forefront of progress in signage requirements from a product's initial design to manufacturing installations and maintenance. An awesome array of CAD workstations today provides detailed drawings to BS.308, a multi-level bill of materials, full colour drawings and 3D modelling. Armed with the most advanced integrated technology in the industry, the company maintains a policy of investment in training and systems that ensures liaison with the client, deals with local authority planning applications, interprets and develops each site scheme, plans and controls projects, and maintains detailed site records.

Considerable investment has been made, particularly in recent years, into the area of computer-programmable metal fabrication equipment, linking it directly with the CAD department. The paint shop provides a range of standard stove enamelled finishes and also offers pearlescent and metallic finishes to automotive industry standards, while products that require extended warranty cover can be provided with Isocyanate based coatings.

Ninety-five percent of the manufacturing processes are carried out on the premises, which gives the company control over costs and ensures that the products are uniform in quality and in finish. Many skills are needed by the experienced workforce, as the fabrication techniques include built-up letters, inlaying, bending and press-moulding in materials such as rigid and foam PVC, acrylics, styrene and MDF. Vinyl graphics are produced using state of the art CNC machines with an extensive selection of fonts, while modern technology deals with the in-house digitising of custom fonts. Neon signs can be provided in an impressive array of 48 different colours.

So what is the secret that has kept Hawes Signs at the cutting edge of the industry for the last 50 years? Clive Hawes believes that it lies in the firm's commitment to an all-round customer service that not only designs and installs signs but includes an ongoing programme of maintenance. He looks forward to the company continuing to provide more of the same over the next half-century!

Top left: *The company's first Northampton factory, in Earl Street.*
Top right: *The company's founder, Mr Kenneth Hawes pictured in 1969.*
Left: *An aerial view of the company as it is today.*

On the road - a company travelling far

World War II had only been over for three years when Frank Blackwell set up his garage in Palmerston Road. The effects of the war were still being felt, and certain goods were still in short supply. This included the motor car, as new cars were being exported as fast as they were made.

Though Britain still had a long way to go before post-war prosperity became a reality for the ordinary family (who travelled by bus!), there were still a large number of mostly pre-war cars about, and Frank Blackwell was perceptive enough to recognise the enormous potential of the motor car. The Palmerston Garage not only offered to supply customers with any make of vehicle but also repaired them and supplied petrol, oil and other motoring accessories.

After Mr Blackwell's death Mr John Bull took over the business in 1962 and four years later he acquired other premises at 68 Denmark Road. This allowed him to diversify while still retaining the garage, and beginning with half a dozen mini-buses he started up a private hire service in October 1966. The company's first coach was a 20-seater mini-coach, acquired in 1971, and a few years later Mr Bull added a 53-seat coach in order to extend the services he could offer. Towards the end of the 1970s he took over three coaches with the accompanying contracts from Overstone.

The continuing success of the venture led the company to invest in a further move in 1980 that took them to St James Mill Road - the firm's current premises. Mr Bull let the original garage business go at this time in order to concentrate on vehicle hire.

The mid 1980s was a time of maximum growth for Country Lion. In a bold move the company branched out into self drive hire, starting with a couple of two-ton vans, one Luton parcel van and a thirty hundredweight tipper truck. Additional land was purchased to extend the hard standing for the increasing number of vehicles.

Below: *The original garage.*

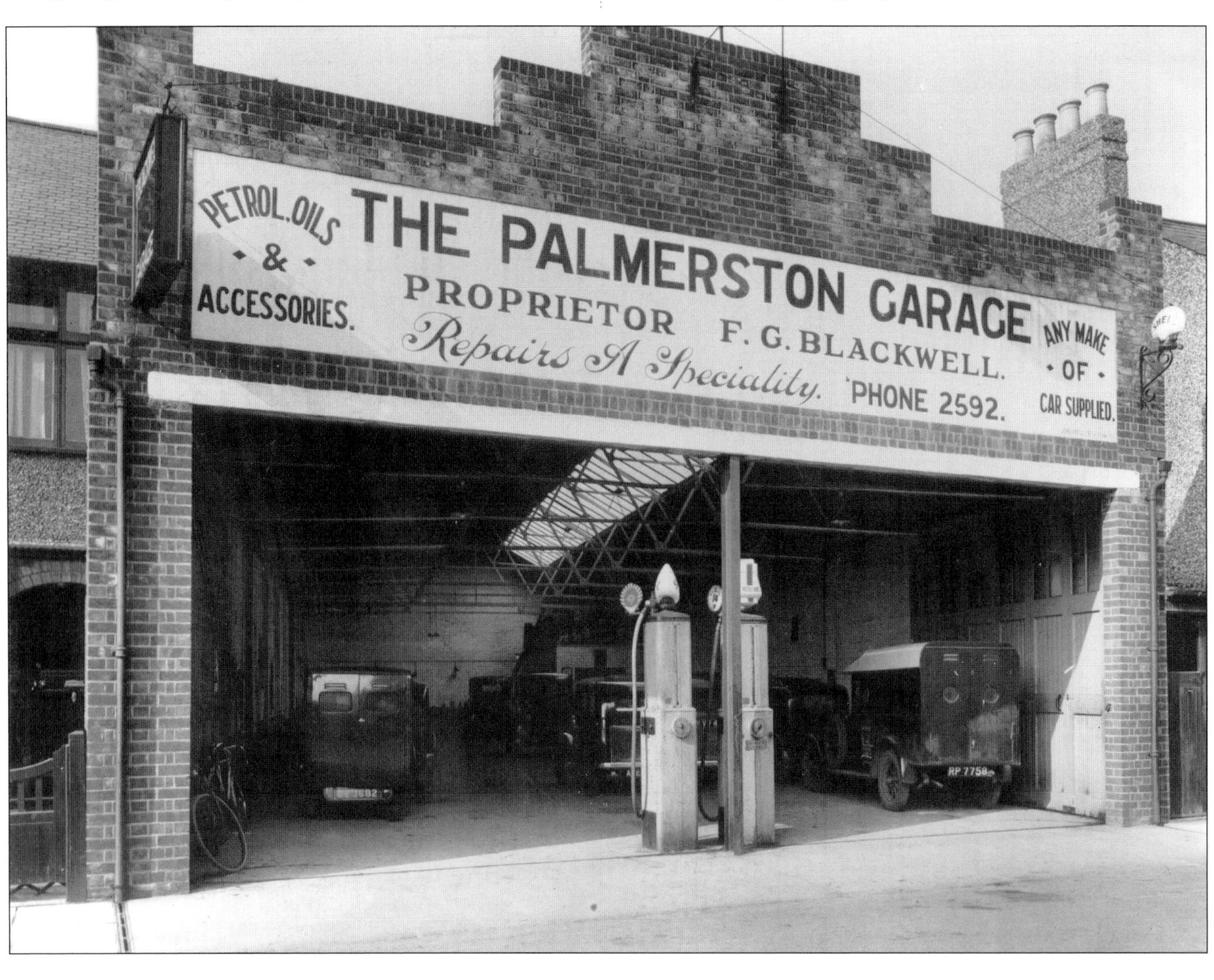

Today the company has a total of 65 self drive vehicles available for hire, including a range of trucks, vans, cars and mini buses.

In 1995 Country Lion continued their expansion by taking over Brittains' coaches together with the related contract work, adding a further eight vehicles to their growing fleet. Today their fleet has an amazing 32 PCV vehicles, from 16-seat mini buses to the latest executive-type coaches that offer clients a relaxing journey complete with videos, fridges, tables and toilets. A dedicated workforce of 35 staff includes, of course, the company's team of competent coach drivers, who are ready to go anywhere, not only in the UK but across the Channel and into Europe.

Nearer home, Country Lion coaches have become a familiar sight on the local roads. Contract work such as the arrangements they have with the Northampton Saints and the Northampton Town team - better known as the Cobblers - is central to the company. Together with the supermarket chain Tesco they provide a much-needed shoppers' bus service. Running from the outlying towns of Milton Keynes, Stony Stratford and Daventry to the Mere Way Superstore, Weston Favell shopping centre and the Wellingborough Tesco store, the coaches stop en-route at around eight or ten pick-up points to collect or drop off passengers.

Education Authority contracts for local schools include transport for Northampton High School for Girls and Wellingborough Boys School, while other works contracts with institutions such as Moulton Agricultural College offer the company further opportunities.

Bus services throughout the town have recently become part of Country Lion's regular work, and aided by a Government Rural Bus Grant they also run a total of three Sunday rural bus services.

On looking back across the last half century, Country Lion has travelled a long way since the days of that first small business in Palmerston Road, in reputation as well as in miles - and hope to continue to offer their services for many years to come.

Top: *The first fleet of mini buses.*
Above: *The company coach of today.*
Right: *Part of the truck and van self-drive hire fleet.*

Gifts of golden memories

The year was 1919; the Great War had ended just the year before and money was tight for Claude and Laurie Jones, a young Northampton couple. The Joneses knew what they wanted from life and that was to own their own business. With a rare determination they went ahead and took the plunge, sinking everything they had into the venture - including their wedding presents, which they sold to raise more capital. Taking their possessions with them - a table, two chairs and a bed - they moved into number 45 Upper Mounts, where they lived above the shop.

Early days

The choice of goods they offered for sale, jewellery, drapery, clothing and a pawnbroker's service, reflected their own retail backgrounds. Claude had been apprenticed to a pawnbroker in Marefair, and had remained with the business until he joined the army as an RAMC sergeant, serving in France. Laurie had worked in a high class ladies' fashion shop until she, too, enlisted for war service. During the war Claude made plans for the future, carefully hoarding his modest sergeant's pay for the business he intended to found.

Once their ambition was realised, the enterprising young couple set about establishing the business, providing a pawnbroking service, much appreciated by needy families in the area, and selling household goods, clothing and jewellery.
In 1923 they were able to employ their first shop assistant.

Depression
Those years of worldwide depression between the wars were difficult and traumatic for Claude and Laurie - they found that their stock had lost half its value overnight. They faced the challenge, however, and survived. More difficulties followed during World War II, when owing to their business being classed as non-essential one of their two members of staff was called upon to be released for war work.

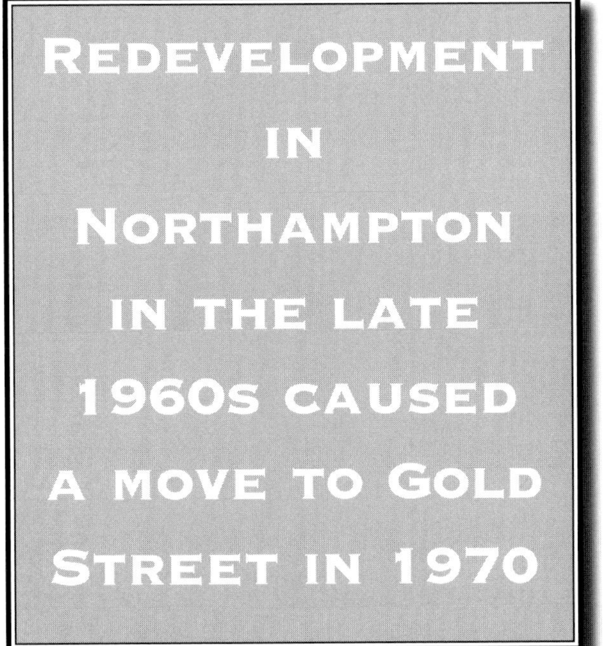

A family concern
One of Claude and Laurie's sons, Michael, grew up to be as ambitious as his father had been, and set about training in the Jewellery Quarter in Birmingham and Ipswich. With National Service behind him, he joined his parents in the business in 1951. Over the next few years Michael improved the business, made alterations to the premises, and employed younger staff.

When a property came up for sale next door but one in Upper Mounts, Michael bought it. Sadly, Claude did not live to see the move made by his son to concentrate entirely on jewellery and associated goods. Michael built a new shop on the nearby site he had purchased, dedicated it to the sale of good class jewellery and watches, and named it Michael Jones Jeweller.

Change
Redevelopment in Northampton in the late 1960s forced the closure of the shops in Upper Mounts. A new town centre shop was opened at One Gold Street in 1970, where Michael Jones quickly established a reputation for quality. In the same year he turned the business into a cooperative - a step of which Michael is justifiably proud - and the business is now owned by its dedicated staff.

Trading from the same address today, the business caters largely for those who want to give beautiful things to others (or to themselves!). Memorable gifts of choice gold jewellery with superior diamonds or coloured gemstones form part of their stock, along with a range of fine watches with such names as Rolex, Cartier, Tag Hueur, Omega, Gucci and Longines. Resident watchmakers and goldsmiths are there to give advice and service.

The company has come a long way since Claude and Laurie opened their first shop. Today's staff are fully trained and have gained appropriate qualifications including Fellowship of the Gemmological Society and Membership of the British Horological Institute.

And what of the future?
Michael Jones looks forward with confidence and determination to a continuing increase in the company's range and choice of merchandise, together with the expertise and qualifications of its staff - all with the aim of being recognised as the best place to buy superior quality gifts that will remain forever special to those who receive them.

Facing page, top: *Claude Samuel Jones 1890-1960.*
Facing page, bottom: *Michael Jones Jeweller - One Gold Street, Northampton.*
Below: *Michael Henry Jones.*

The boots that fly

The Company which was later to become Haynes & Cann was incorporated on 18th August, 1919 as Youngents Ltd, making youths footwear and also special clothing for motorists.

Founded by Mr FS Haynes and Mr E C Warren, the firm started production in a factory in Ethel Street, Northampton.

The Cuirass Auto-Vest manufactured by Youngents was the winter garment to be seen in back in 1919, especially if you were the driver of one of those magnificent but draughty early motor cars. The lambswool-lined waistcoats were, as their advertisement stressed, a clever idea. With no front opening to let in the cold air, the snug leather vests could be slipped on and fastened without even taking off your overcoat. And the price of this ingenious invention? Fifteen shillings, including the leather wallet to keep the vest neat and tidy when not in use. In today's currency (if not in value) seventy-five pence!

Youngents Ltd also manufactured a range of footwear. The change from youths to men's footwear came gradually, but by 1930 the company was concentrating entirely on shoes and boots for men. The same year saw the change of name of the firm to Haynes & Cann Ltd. Mr Archie Haynes, son of one of the founders, joined the company at the outset after completing service in the Royal Flying Corps during the first world war, an association which continued until 1984 when he retired as Managing Director. Another long term association with the company began in 1929 with the recruitment of Miss May Pettifer whose family ran an ironmongers shop in Earl Street. What started off as a temporary position extended to 55 years!

In 1930, Mr Percy Cann, the son of the by then co-owner, joined the company. Mr Percy Cann went on to become Lord Mayor of Bristol in 1949.

1937 was a key year; Mr Percy Cann left the company and Mr Ron Kitchin arrived to partner Archie Haynes, an association which was to continue until 1960 when Ron departed to join SATRA- the Kettering based Shoe & Allied Trades Research Association. During their years together Archie Haynes' role was mainly one of selling, in which he spent most of his time on the road, while Ron Kitchin developed new products and managed the manufacturing operation.

Archie Haynes' service in military intelligence during the second world war led to a suggestion, in 1940, from which Ron Kitchin developed the famous 'Escape' boot for the RAF. This was a design which enabled aircrews who baled out over enemy-held territory to cut off the leg of the upper leaving a shoe section which was sufficiently normal in appearance to assist them to escape detection. This was the start of a link with military footwear for the flying services which has extended to the present. From that point, the Company continued to make boots for military aircrew alongside women's footwear; women's winter boots becoming a speciality. The production of women's footwear continued until about the mid 1960s since which time the Company has devoted itself almost entirely to specialist military footwear for the flying services.

***Above** centre: The 'Auto-vest', the lambswool waistcoat patented by the company. **Left:** Mr Archie Haynes shortly before his retirement in 1984 with some of the boots in production at that time.*

The company had remained in Ethel Street until it was teamed with the Bective Shoe Company for the duration of the second world war. During the war, closing rooms were also set up in Yardley Hastings in Northamptonshire and in Eastbourne. In 1946 they moved to Hood Street until 1959 when they entered into a nomadic period moving in with Arnold Bros in Talbot Road in 1961, then moving in with Queen Shoes in Henry Street and in 1963 moving in with Pollard & Son in St Michael's Road where they stayed until 1984. During this period, 1959-1984, Haynes & Cann utilised the production facilities of the companies with which they were co-habiting.

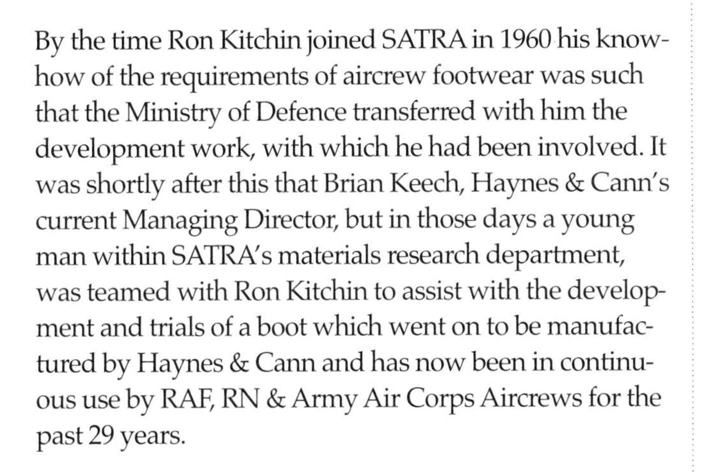

By the time Ron Kitchin joined SATRA in 1960 his know-how of the requirements of aircrew footwear was such that the Ministry of Defence transferred with him the development work, with which he had been involved. It was shortly after this that Brian Keech, Haynes & Cann's current Managing Director, but in those days a young man within SATRA's materials research department, was teamed with Ron Kitchin to assist with the development and trials of a boot which went on to be manufactured by Haynes & Cann and has now been in continuous use by RAF, RN & Army Air Corps Aircrews for the past 29 years.

By 1984, having reached the age of 84, Managing Director Archie Haynes decided he would like to retire and sell the business at which time it was taken over by a consortium comprising of Brian Keech, Brian Smith and Roger Starmer. Also at that time the Company took over the direct manufacture of its products which, for some years past, had been manufactured under sub-contract. Also in that same year of 1984 the Company moved premises to the refurbished first floor of the old Brevitt factory building on the corner of Overstone Road and Clare Street, creating better conditions for the work force, and providing space for expansion. Shortly after moving in, the Company was privileged to have a visit from HRH The Duke of Gloucester in his capacity as Patron of the Worshipful Company of Pattenmakers.

In recent years the Company's Quality Systems have been developed and the Company is currently registered as complying with the requirements of BS EN ISO 9001: 1994 for its Production and Development capabilities and to Defence Standard 05 -123/I for its Design ability. In addition to military Aircrew boots, boots for Crash Fire Crews and boots for Parachute Jumping Instructors, the Company has developed a capability for the manufacture of fabric flying helmets and the associated ear capsules and for the manufacture of aircrew survival hoods. An increasing amount of development work has also been carried out under contract to the UK MoD and, in addition, the Company has linked up with others in the aerospace field to assist in the development of complete life support systems for particularly demanding situations. This has provided the opportunity for Brian Keech to observe at first hand, and sometimes to actually experience himself, the hazards to which some of the equipment is subjected.

Above: *HRH The Duke of Gloucester GVCO visiting the company in its new premises at the corner of Overstone Road and Clare Street in March 1985 in his capacity of Patron of the Worshipful Company of Pattenmakers.*

The UK Ministry of Defence is the principal customer for the Company's products, but major aircraft manufacturers and many overseas Air Forces are also important customers.

The Aircrew boots which are currently produced in the largest numbers embody features such that they are compatible with the other special clothing which needs to be worn when flying modern high performance military aircraft while allowing the wearer to operate comfortably, effectively and with maximum efficiency. In addition to fulfilling the necessary requirements for normal flying duties, the boots possess the qualities to enable the wearer to survive in a hostile environment in an emergency. There is a constant awareness that a feature or a minor deficiency which may only be a nuisance in footwear for more mundane applications could have disastrous consequences when flying a high performance aircraft or when trying to survive in an emergency situation.

Ninety years in fine leathers

A bicycle and a hired hand truck formed the entire 'fleet' of vehicles used by the three partners in a small leather business when it began back in 1908.

W Pearce & Co was established by Mr C A Pearce, Mr C J Pearce and Mr W G Pearce in a room in Burns Street, which they rented for a weekly rent of two shillings and sixpence. The business started in a small way, cutting leather shoe linings for local footwear companies and buying and selling leather, and Pearce's staff consisted of two young boys.

As time went on, a steady re-investment into the company and the staff's hard work paid off. With the expansion came the move, in 1912, to larger premises in Victoria Road. Five years later a second building was purchased in St Edmunds Road nearby. With the outbreak of World War I came a change of direction. The War Office needed sheepskin leather clothing for the military, which led to the company establishing itself as a leather manufacturer. By 1919 W Pearce & Co was producing a number of speciality leathers, and after the war export markets were sought for their products. A visit to an international exhibition in Lyons led to the setting up of their first overseas agent in France. By 1925 Pearce's had become the swiftest expanding company of its kind in the country. During the same year the firm became a Private Limited Liability Company, appointing Mr HA Skinner, who had joined the firm as an office boy thirteen years earlier, to the board.

The company survived the years of worldwide depression in the 1920s and early 30s, and by 1934 was thriving. Production, however, was spread across five separate factories, and the board realised the inefficiencies of this way of working. They decided to continue their policy of expansion and began looking for larger premises. A suitable site near Billing was found, which is today the site of the

Above left: *Burns Street from where the factory originally started in 1908.* ***Below:*** *The administration block in 1939.* ***Bottom:*** *The staff at the opening of the new factory in 1939.*

tannery. New innovations and methods of production were pioneered by the company's research department around the same time; pleated effects, two-colour suede and the use of lithography on leather were developed and adopted. Further markets were established abroad, and the subsidiary company, Pearce and Friedman, was set up in New York.

June 1st 1939 saw the official opening of the new tannery, and around 500 customers, suppliers, competitors, staff and employees attended the ceremony, which was performed by the Bishop of Peterborough. A few short months later the outbreak of the second world war put paid to the firm's plans for expanding production in the new premises. Output was maintained however, in spite of the loss of many employees to the military. Once more the emphasis within the company changed, and though a small amount of fashion leather was still produced the main demand was for service footwear, clothes and equipment. The war years were difficult ones for Pearce's, and the rationing of supplies and an acute shortage of raw materials called for a great deal of ingenuity.

The post-war years held further difficulties for the company; many of their pre-war outlets were now behind the Iron Curtain and were inaccessible to trade. The directors immediately began to study and assess potential new markets abroad. With the 1960s came the direct threat posed by the increasing use of synthetic materials in the shoe industry; this led to Pearce's diversifying into the production of other leather goods which would not be so greatly affected by the use of synthetics. At the same time a shortage of labour in the Northampton area brought about the company's investment in modern labour-saving machinery.

This was only the beginning of the great things that were to come. In recent years significant investments have been made in new machinery, buildings, boilers, combined heat and power plant and research into the latest developments in technology, ensuring a constant supply of high specification, water resistant and innovative fashion leathers. Stringent laboratory testing and ISO 9002 accreditation underline the quality of Pearce's products, and brand-named customers worldwide form an important part of the company's markets for quality leather footwear, handbags, book bindings and other leather goods.

After 90 years of experience and dedication to the production of fine leathers, Pearce's plan is to continue to build on their technical superiority in future years. Their intention is to carry on producing distinctive leather for the next 90 years.

Top: *An early view of the power station.*
Above left: *An aerial view of the tannery in 1939.*
Below: *The crust warehouse.*

The children of Stimpson Avenue School collect their Coronation souvenirs in June 1953.

ACKNOWLEDGMENTS

The publishers would like to thank Alan Burman for providing many of the photographs within this book, and also for his help in the course of research and proof-reading.

Thanks are also due to Peter Thomas who penned the editorial captions.